RIG

AN ORAL HISTORY OF THE
OCEAN RANGER
DISASTER

Mike Heffernan's Rig *is a moving elegy for the 84 men who died on the* Ocean Ranger *and an indictment of the horrendous labour conditions that made the disaster inevitable.* Rig *is a powerful and important book.*
– Lisa Moore, author of
Alligator and *Open*

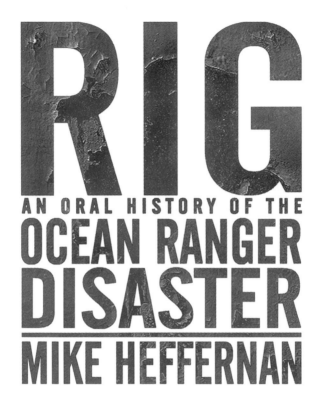

RIG

AN ORAL HISTORY OF THE
OCEAN RANGER
DISASTER

MIKE HEFFERNAN

CREATIVE PUBLISHERS

St. John's, Newfoundland and Labrador
2009

We gratefully acknowledge the financial support of the Canada Council for the Arts, the Government of Canada through the Book Publishing Industry Development Program (BPIDP), and the Government of Newfoundland and Labrador through the Department of Tourism, Culture and Recreation for our publishing program.

Layout by Todd Manning

Printed on acid-free paper

Published by
CREATIVE PUBLISHERS
an imprint of CREATIVE BOOK PUBLISHING
a Transcontinental Inc. associated company
P.O. Box 8660, Station A
St. John's, Newfoundland and Labrador A1B 3T7

Printed in Canada by:
TRANSCONTINENTAL INC.

Library and Archives Canada Cataloguing in Publication

Heffernan, Mike, 1978-
    Rig : an oral history of the Ocean Ranger disaster / Mike Heffernan.

ISBN 978-1-897174-41-8

    1. Ocean Ranger (Drilling rig). 2. Drilling platforms–Accidents–Newfoundland and Labrador. 3. Offshore oil well drilling–Accidents–Newfoundland and Labrador. 4. Disaster victims–Family relationships–Newfoundland Labrador. 5. Marine accidents–Social aspects–Newfoundland and Labrador. 6. Oral history–Newfoundland and Labrador. I. Title.

TN871.3.H43 2009   363.11'96223381909718   C2009-900268-X

*To my mother, for keeping his memory alive...
and the 84 crewmen of the drill rig* Ocean Ranger
who lost their lives on February 15, 1982.

Wisely and slow; they stumble that run fast.
– William Shakespeare,
Romeo and Juliet

Truth and oil always come to the surface.
– Spanish proverb

CONTENTS

Historical Note 1

Prologue: What Our Children Have Lost 5

PART ONE: MADHOUSE

DAVE RUSSELL
The Most Dangerous Part of the Rig 13

ROBERT ST. AUBIN
About Things Not Looking Good 19

JOHN CROWE
About Getting a Break 23

LARRY BRAZIL
About An Ornery Kind of Guy 29

OSCAR HEANEY
Heading Towards Disaster 33

LLOYD MAJOR
About Some Stuff Not Being True 38

WANDA FRAMPTON
Memories That Will Last Forever,
But Which Will Make Me Sad Forever 42

GARY WALL
The 85th Man 46

Swearing: A Postscript 49

PART TWO: THE CASUALTY

MIKE COLE
About Staring Out Over the Rail 55

RICK FLYNN
About the Drill Continually Turning Right 59

JERRY HIGDON
About Not Believing 62

THOMAS KANE
About Where We Were and Where We're At Now 67

PATRICK FAHEY
About Feeling Bloody Useless 73

CRIS SONNTAG
The Darkness of a Little House 77

WAYDE BUTLER
The Worst Week of My Life 83

CARL STAUBITZER
About Looking and Looking and Looking 89

MAX RUELOKKE
The Depths of the Rig 94

PART THREE: DAY OF RECKONING

BARBARA YAFFE AND GERRY PHELAN
Two Monologues About Being Young 100

SUSAN SHERK
Responsibility and Regret 107

RAY HAWCO
About It Never Being Easy 112

GARY BROWNE
About Barely Catching Your Breath 117

REV. BERT CHEESEMAN
Those Families That I Knew Personally 122

MARIE WADDEN
About a Witness 127

PART FOUR: THE LONGEST WEEK

ANNMARI
About Being the First 135

ELAINE
A Unique Bond 139

CONNIE
About Seeing Him That Last Time 147

SANDRA
About an Absolute Void 153

TRACEY
About the Next One to Go 158

EVELYN
About Being Proud of Your Son 163

PATRICIA
About Sticking Together Through the Worst of It 169

DON
Going Quiet 175

CLE NEWHOOK
Drawing a Line Across That Year 179

PART FIVE: A SMALL MEASURE OF COMFORT

ROBERT STRONG
About a Gratifying Feeling 187

BRIAN
Why Remembering is Still So Important 193

Epilogue, or About Finding Courage 198

Acknowledgements 203

HISTORICAL NOTE

When it was launched in 1976, the Ocean Ranger *was the largest, self-pro-pelled semi-submersible offshore drilling unit in the world. Designed by ODECO Engineers Incorporated for ODECO International of New Orleans, Louisiana, and the Norwegian firm of Fernley & Eger A/S, it was built at the Hiroshima yard of Mitsubishi Heavy Industries. The rig's maiden voyage in June of that year led from Japan to Alaska. After completing wells in the Bering Sea, the Gulf of Alaska, and the Lower Cook Inlet, it left that area in September 1977 and remained idle, moored at various locations on the west coast of North America until August 1979. The rig was then moved east via Cape Horn to drill a well in the Baltimore Canyon off New Jersey, thence to Ireland in May 1980 for another two wells, and finally back across the Atlantic to arrive on the Grand Banks of Newfoundland on November 6, 1980. The* Ocean Ranger *began drilling in the Hibernia Field on contract between Mobil Oil Canada Limited, the operator for the Hibernia Consortium, and ODECO Drilling of Canada Limited. This contract, signed in February 1980, was initially for thirteen months, but after its expiry a two-year agreement was negotiated and accepted by both parties. Under this contract, ODECO was responsible for the rig and the crew, and Mobil was responsible for the well.*

– Report One: The Loss of the
Semi-submersible Drill Rig *Ocean Ranger* and its Crew;
Royal Commission on the *Ocean Ranger* Maritime Disaster

Eighty-four men are missing and feared lost after one of the world's biggest oil rigs, the Ocean Ranger, *sank today in a howling North Atlantic gale in the Hibernia oil exploration area off Newfoundland.*

Mobil Oil Canada, which operated the rig, said bodies were spotted in the water where the rig had been operating, 175 nautical miles east of St. John's. In an official statement about nine hours after the rig crew was ordered to abandon ship, Mobil said the rig had gone down. It had been battered by overnight winds and was listing badly for hours.

Rescue planes and ships battled poor visibility in rain and snow, as well as icy conditions, in attempts to locate survivors.

If all hands have been lost, it will be the worst marine disaster in decades off the Canadian east coast and by far the worst in a string of ship disasters this winter. It would also mark the first multiple loss of life off an oil rig in Eastern Canadian waters.

Mobil's brief statement said that Air-Sea Rescue has been unable to locate the Ocean Ranger, *but the site has been identified by helicopter through the rig's anchor buoys and wave-rider buoys. This equipment would have been attached to the drill rig itself and would pinpoint the drill site.*

Two lifeboats were sighted by search aircraft, one capsized and the other stern-down in the water. A partially inflated liferaft also was seen by search and rescue helicopters that are at the site along with a Buffalo aircraft.

– "Rig Goes Down; Bodies Sighted"
in *The Evening Telegram*, February 15, 1982

By now the chain of events is a familiar one: a broken porthole window in the ballast control room, seawater on the ballast panel, an untrained crew unable to remedy the problem, a pump system that failed to help right the tilting rig, a failure to ensure watertight compartments in crucial areas, like the anchor chain lockers, and lifeboats that smashed like eggshells in the angry North Atlantic storm. The report confirms that all of this contributed to the loss of the rig and its 84-man crew.

Everyone gets some blame: the Federal and Provincial governments for having inadequate legislative control offshore, the oil companies, Mobil and ODECO, for not providing proper training and life-saving equipment for the rig's crew, and agencies like the US Coast Guard and Search and Rescue. Everyone gets some blame, largely for their lack of foresight that a marine tragedy of this magnitude could ever have occurred.

– Marie Wadden, CBC News: *Here & Now*,
August 13, 1984

War and work cost a lot in Newfoundland. They always have. The Ocean Ranger *disaster flashed through the circuits of these common memories connected with them, but with an additional irony. The offshore was not the seal hunt or the ancient fishery. Oil was modern. The rig was a splendour of engineering and technology. The jobs belonged to an industry that might walk us away from dependency and from those old, harsh patterns of hard times and inescapable perils. The offshore was for many Newfoundlanders all hope and future, but here we were on February 15, 1982, in the last quarter of the gleam-ing twentieth century about to veer into a new, more accommodating richer encounter with the sea and its resources, and that terrible bell rang once again. Families hurled into grief, communities lacerated, the whole province once again struggling to absorb an assault too large for anything but time or faith to carry. Twenty-five years on, it is, of course, still being felt.*

– Rex Murphy, CBC News: *The National,*
February 15, 2007

Clyde Parsons and his two children, Nancy and Richard. Written on the back of the photo: "First and last Christmas dinner."

PROLOGUE: WHAT OUR CHILDREN HAVE LOST
Cynthia, a wife

What do I remember? I remember an awful fear. I feared the future. I feared for what was going to happen to our two children.

All Clyde ever wanted was to provide for them. But before he went offshore, we struggled. He was a body mechanic and got laid off and we sold our house in St. Phillips to buy something cheaper in Foxtrap. I was a nursing assistant and needed to go back to work if we were going to get by.

Clyde got the job roughnecking through begging and begging and banging on doors. In the end, someone he knew helped him out, maybe someone in the family—I can't quite remember. He was so thrilled to have it, to be working again.

He didn't like it much out there, the politics of the ship, the Americans. He had his mind made up that he was going to work and keep his nose clean and not get involved in anything because of what it meant for us. But I never did worry over him. It was the *Ocean Ranger*. Everyone in the industry knew that it was the best, or thought that it was the best, and I never once heard him say there was something wrong out there. The kids were certainly too young to think about it. To them, Daddy was gone to work.

With him making so much more money, I could stay home, which was something he really wanted. We started to pay off the house. We saved money in a little fund set up to take the kids to Disney World. It felt good to plan for the future instead of living hand-to-mouth.

Some of the other wives resented the three weeks apart; we were determined to make it work. While he was gone, I did everything around the house that needed getting done, so that when he got home we could spend all of our time together. If the kids wanted to play, he could play. He could get down on the floor and play with them for hours and hours. The four of us could. He was a musician and spent a lot of time with them singing. We were campers and often went to the park. We could do all sorts of things together.

That last time I saw him is still there, in my memory. It'll always be there. I remember him kissing the kids goodbye. I remember him going down over the stairs. I remember him looking back, his face. Why he did that, I don't know. It hit me right then: *What if anything should ever happen to him?* I never thought of that before, some kind of fear. I remember the bedroom window was frosted over. I tried to see him backing out. I tried to wave goodbye.

A storm started to come up on Sunday, Valentine's Day. My father called and wanted us to come down and spend the night. Along the way we stopped, and the kids bought Clyde a card and some partridge-berry jam. Nancy and her father had their own little something ready for me in a drawer in her bedroom.

The phone rang early Monday morning. My brother, Peter, answered. "What rig is Clyde on?" he asked me.

"The *Ocean Ranger*," I told him.

"Cynthia, I think you'd better come to the phone."

It was my sister, Carol. She'd heard something on the radio, something about the men taking to the lifeboats. Something serious had happened out there.

I think I must've screamed.

The kids were asking, "What's wrong? What's wrong?"

My mother said, "You have to stay calm. The children are watching you, and you have to be careful. You're going to frighten them. You're their mother, and you have to stay calm."

That's what I did. I became another person.

By eight o'clock, the entire family had come through the door.

My older brother, Lloyd, took over. He went to the ODECO office in St. John's looking for information, some information, any information. No one would speak to him. The doors were locked and a notice put up. He was very angry.

My brother-in-law, a fisherman, didn't think there would be any survivors. "It's not going to work, it's not going to work," he kept repeating. "He's not coming back."

Clyde's parents came by. In their hearts and in their souls, they, too, felt that he was gone.

Being young and naïve, I still had hope. "They're alive, somewhere."

By the afternoon, it was announced the rig had sunk.

That night, when the names came on the news and then the video of the capsized lifeboat, I knew that he wasn't coming home to us. I knew then. It was all like looking through a window, like it was some-one else's life. It was unreal.

On the second day, we hoped for a body. That was important; I wanted that, for closure. We waited the whole week. Every time the phone rang, we expected it to be the call. But it never came.

My great-aunt said, "That's God's will. There's a reason for all of this." That upset me. My husband, the father of my children, was gone forever. How could that be God's will? How could the loss of eighty-four men be God's will?

Reverend Coffin reassured me: "My child, that isn't God's will. Accidents happen and disasters happen. That is man's doing, not God's will."

We held a memorial service in St. Phillips. I didn't take the kids because I thought they were too young: Richard was just four and Nancy was eight.

I thought I was doing right by protecting them. It was a mistake. When I talk to them now, especially Nancy, they say that I protected them too much, that they should've been there with me. I was just trying to make sure they weren't hurt more than they already were.

Maybe I should've known. My family tried to protect me in the same way, and I felt smothered. When the *Ocean Ranger* Families Foundation started up, I wanted to go to that first meeting. They said, "What do you want to go to that for? You're torturing yourself." They didn't even want me to read the papers, didn't want me watching the news.

Then there were the feelings bottled up within me, growing.

It was hard seeing Clyde's family. They were very musical, and I couldn't bear to hear music because it reminded me of him. It was a long time before I could hear music without getting emotional—years and years. Even now, it can get hold of me, certain things.

It was lying alone at night when everything came out. The lifeboat was always in the back of my mind, the one that was never found. I knew it was foolishness, but I just couldn't let go. *Was there anyone in it? Was Clyde in it?*

Those things were there when I met George.

I remember I didn't want to be by myself. I was still hurt but knew I had to go on without Clyde. I thought, *How can I possibly want someone else in my life after such a short time? What if he returns and I'm with another man?* I thought about that a lot. It made me sad. Maybe I thought I needed a father for my children. But it was impossible for anyone to ever fill Clyde's shoes.

I don't think I've ever told those things to anyone before—maybe my sister.

I could see what Clyde's death had done to the kids.

As Nancy grew older, she never spoke of the *Ocean Ranger*. She didn't want to talk about it, didn't want to hear about it. She had her memories and I would say to her, "Nancy, you never talk about your father. You don't have any pictures of him in your bedroom."

"I don't want to." It was all that she could say.

It wasn't until she got married when she realized her father wasn't going to be there. That was the turning point. She changed after that, had more acceptance. From time to time, I would even hear her speak of him.

But what does a four-year-old remember?

Friends of ours had home movies of birthday parties and holidays we'd shared. They decided, with Nancy opening up, they'd make a video to play at her wedding. We even found a tape of her father singing and included that, too.

I walked in on Richard watching it for the first time. He was crying. "I've never seen him walk," he told me.

That's what a four-year-old remembers, a lifetime...

A lifetime of being without his father.

PART I

MADHOUSE

We are talking about the type of lads who chase money, the kind of lads who are prepared to go up to the north of Scotland and work on hydroelectric stations for maybe four months without getting home or anything like that because they've got a target of £2,000 or £3,000 in mind.

– Senior official,
British Government; Department of
Energy, Petroleum Engineering Division

You get the odd toolpusher who is genuinely concerned about the men's welfare, but they are few and far between.

– Anonymous roughneck, from WG Carson,
The Other Price of Britain's Oil

Safety?

– Miner Jack Callaghan, from Elliott Leyton,
Dying Hard: The Ravages of Industrial Carnage

The *Ocean Ranger* while en route from Hiroshima to Alaska. Shortly before ODECO closed its doors in April 1983, the photo hung in their St. John's office. It was given to Dave Russell by Blondie Gernandt, the onshore manager.

THE MOST DANGEROUS PART OF THE RIG
Dave Russell; Roustabout, ODECO

I n the early winter of 1979, I had an interview with Kelvin "Blondie" Gernandt, Operations Manager for the Ocean Drilling and Exploration Company. Four hundred other guys were there and I was the only one with a shirt and tie on. Thinking back, it must've made a difference.

When I went into his office, Blondie, wearing a cowboy hat and boots, pointed to a picture of a semi-submersible behind his desk and said in a thick southern drawl, "That's ma rig. I built that rig. What kind of job do you want on ma rig, a radio operator or a roustabout?" Figuring I could get up on the drill floor, I signed on as a roustabout. I was supposed to receive a call from John MacIntyre, the onshore materials man, and waited weeks for a reply. Finally, I decided to call him instead. He said, to my surprise, "You should've gone out this morning." I left on the next chopper, the second from St. John's to the *Ocean Ranger*. That was in November 1980.

The office was a madhouse. ODECO was hiring people right off the street with no formal training or orientation and bringing them out to the rig. But the most dangerous part wasn't the structure of the rig or the equipment, but the operation itself and the American supervisors running the show: Kent Thompson, the Mobil toolpusher; Jimmy Counts, ODECO's rig superintendent; and Bill Dugas, the crane operator.

They could make or break you.

For the entire fifteen months the *Ranger* was here, Newfoundlanders were shit on severely—there was no respect. Because the guys would be so fed up with being treated like dogs, I'd go out after three weeks of being ashore and there would be a whole new crew of roughnecks and roustabouts. There would be wind and rain and snow and sleet, and you would try to measure pipe to get it up on the catwalk so the drillers could make the connection, and the derrickman would be cursing you down to the dirt. One time, four roustabouts were waiting on a chopper, and I was at the bottom of the stairs leading to the helideck. Bill and Buddy Ferguson, the subsea engineer, were there, too. Bill said, "It looks like the chopper isn't going to land. The

Newfoundland Air Force is blocking the helideck." I climbed up and saw that there were seagulls everywhere. The Americans all started laughing.

There were two brothers from Torbay, both roughnecks. For whatever reason, Jimmy ran one of them off the drill floor. Early the next morning, the older one went into Jimmy's bedroom, flicked on the light and gave it to him. He did Jimmy up real proper. We didn't see him for a long time afterwards, maybe ten days. When the next supply boat arrived, Bill was up in the crane and called for the two brothers to come out so he could lower them down. When they got in the personnel basket all they had on were jeans and light jackets. This was the middle of winter—it was freezing and the wind was going. He took them up real high, at least a hundred feet from the water, and held them out there for forty-five minutes. They didn't say a word; they knew why they were there. I remember coming out of the main office and watching all of this. Jimmy would've told Bill to *get them the fuck off the rig*, and I'm sure they had a real good laugh about it afterwards. Bill was generally a hard man to deal with. He'd be up in the crane and get on the horn and really berate people over the PA. So, if he had a beef with you that day and called you every name under the sun, including *a dumb fucking Newfie*, everyone would hear it.

One time I cornered him, wanting to know how many guys he had "run off." He told me just four Brits, but that he'd made life so miserable for a lot of others that they just up and quit, anyway. That's how ODECO got rid of God knows how many Newfoundlanders.

We weren't accustomed to that kind of attitude. I used to say to the guys, "If you were in St. John's working as a janitor you'd make minimum wage of two dollars an hour. You're getting ten times that out here doing the same job. Just try and bite your tongue." A lot of them couldn't understand that, and it usually meant their job.

Before I went into Materials, I was a lead roustabout. I would come in a few minutes early and tell the guys on the night shift what I wanted done, and we'd discuss what had gone on that day. But no one was ever sure what they were doing, and accidents were common.

People were breaking arms and losing fingers. Steve Windsor came to me two days after arriving and said he was going up on the drill floor. At the time, roughnecks were getting fifty cents more an hour than roustabouts. I warned him: "You've only been out here a few days—you don't know the equipment, the tools, the terminology, the people or the operation. Wait a few hitches." Later that day, he got his hand mashed and lost a few fingers.

Ron Foley and Michael Maurice were untying bulk hoses from the portside railing. When Ron pulled back he fell between the deck and the grading. Michael just swung around, grabbed his leg with one hand and held him dangling until Bill got down off the crane and helped him pull Ron back up. If he had fallen he would've bounced off one of the columns—he wouldn't have survived. I came out the next morning and was told what had happened. Ron was white as a sheet.

For a while, we were in need of a crane operator, and a guy came up from New Orleans to work the graveyard shift. The first thing he did was beat the windsock off with the personnel basket. Another time he broke the windows out of the crane cage with a cargo container. I told the guys not to have anything to do with him, he was trouble. It turned out he was just a roustabout who had conned his way into the job. He'd never operated a crane before in his life.

During my time off, I worked at the ODECO office on Topsail Road. I was privy to a lot of things the other guys weren't, and it became obvious to me that the rig supervisors were trying to cut costs at any expense. We didn't have survival suits, just a few dozen asbestos helicopter suits the whole crew shared and which were commonly referred to as "body bags." Through the course of a few hundred trips the material got worn, and when you put your boot down the leg it would go straight through the side. They needed to be replaced. Down in the motor room, I explained to Kent we had to order new ones. He turned to me and said, "Dave, there's sixteen thousand people looking for your job." I told him thanks and walked out.

The Saturday before the *Ranger* went down, at about six in the morning, John Wilson, a welder, was fixing the brackets on the #1 lifeboat. I was there getting him welding leads and coffee and I happened to look at the railing in relation to the horizon. It was obvious we had a list. Right away I went into Jack Jacobsen's office, the new toolpusher Mobil had sent over from *Sedco 706*. "There's a problem on deck. We're not right—it doesn't feel right. We're listing too far to the portside."

The alarm was sounded and we got everyone up and moved them to the muster stations. I was responsible for the forward lifeboat. After a head count, I realized one guy was missing; I had to go get him. Before I did, I said to John Crowe, the assistant crane operator, "Don't you leave this fucking rig without me!"

Below deck, no one had heard the alarm. There were about a dozen foghorn speakers right off the drill floor that went all through the rig via the PA, including the accommodation rooms. The supervisors wouldn't turn them down, so we'd either disconnect them or stuff something in there to muffle the noise.

I went through the Moonpool, the control room, out through the sack room and into the cement room. The missing man was in there scrubbing the floors and didn't have a clue anything was going on. When I got back up, the Schlumberger guys weren't there, either. The three of them had been up for two days straight doing some kind of test on the well and were probably sleeping through the whole thing. The steward, who was supposed to get everyone out of bed and onto the deck, was coming up the stairs when I was running back down. He was only a young kid. I grabbed him by the arm and told him to look through the rooms on one side while I checked the others. As soon as I turned my back, he took off up the stairs. Luckily, I found the Schlumberger guys right where I thought they'd be, in their bunks.

The list was corrected and we had what could be loosely described as a "safety meeting" in the recreation room. Jimmy was there, as well as a safety engineer from Louisiana. He was explaining what had happened when Jimmy cut in. "Don't forget, ya'll—this rig can't sink." He then walked out.

I worked on the *Ranger* right from square one, but I never once looked inside a lifeboat, not until that Saturday afternoon. On Sundays, we would have our safety exercise. You would finish your dinner, get your lifejacket, wait for the horn to sound and then just stand around, smoke a cigarette and have a little bullshit session. But you didn't get in the lifeboat or start the motor. When I left the *Ranger*, I went on the *Zapata Ugland*. First thing, the captain brought me up and sat me in a lifeboat and showed me everything I needed to know. Nobody showed us anything on the *Ranger*.

***

I got home the following Thursday.

That Monday morning I was out running a few errands and was stopped at Irving on Torbay Road when I heard over the radio that the rig had sunk and all hands were presumed lost. I turned around and went straight for the office. Even then, reporters were gathering at the locked front door. John MacIntyre was there and we spoke for a few minutes. Then Jimmy walked in and went straight upstairs, his head hung low. It might've been 8:30 in the morning. He had gone out to the rig site that night and was just returning. He never mentioned what he saw.

A MONOLOGUE ABOUT THINGS NOT LOOKING GOOD
Robert St. Aubin; Ice and Weather Observer, MacLaren Plansearch

My brother-in-law was going to an interview for a job offshore as an ice and weather observer with MacLaren Plansearch when his car broke down. Since I just lived up the road, I gave him a lift. While I waited, the receptionist asked if I'd like to fill out an application. "Sure," I said, "I've got nothing better to do."

The next day they called and I ended up getting hired.

With just the minimum two weeks of training, I was sent offshore to *Zapata Ugland* and later transferred to *Sedco 706*.

In early February, the company sent me to the *Ocean Ranger* to fill in for a guy who'd gone out West. It was the first time I'd been on that particular rig.

When we landed, I was met by the safety man. My introduction was brief: "Here's your room. Down the hall and up the door is the lifeboat station." My father had a marina for thirty-plus years; I grew up around boats, and safety was always a priority. On *Zapata Ugland*, which had an experienced Norwegian marine crew, we were constantly drilled about safety and standards were very high. When you got in a survival suit they'd actually stand there with a stopwatch to see how long it took you to put it on. Safety was a big concern on *Sedco 706*, too. Right off, I was a little uneasy aboard the *Ranger*.

Early Saturday morning, I had my feet up reading a book and all of a sudden the abandon boat alarm sounded. I thought it was an odd time to have a drill. Although we hadn't had one that previous week, I knew they were held at one o'clock on Sunday afternoons. Looking out the window, I could see men moving quickly, and when I got up it felt like I was standing on one of those amusement park attractions with the tilting floors. I thought, *This isn't right—something is definitely wrong*. I put on my boots and every bit of clothing I had, including a lifejacket and hard hat, and went to the muster station adjacent the pilothouse. Men were already there and lifejackets were being passed around, but there were still about ten or fifteen guys who didn't have one—there simply weren't enough. At one point, I even considered going back for the three we had. What really struck me was the fact that it was the middle of February and there were twenty guys in just

jeans and T-shirts, no hats or coats or gloves. It's the North Atlantic—
it's cold, it's minus one with forty-five knot winds. Those guys were just
about frozen. Then the motor on the lifeboat wouldn't start. They
tried and tried and tried, but it just wouldn't start. I was later told by a
regular crew member that they once got in and tried to lower it, but
that it wouldn't go down and that the seat buckles were rusted and
seized. The safety engineer counted sixty-three men. There was no
way everyone was going to fit in there. I remember saying, looking at
a lifeboat sitting on the deck waiting to be installed, "This doesn't look
good. I don't like this at all."

It seemed like a long, long time before the rig finally came back.

The supervisors called off the emergency and told everyone to
meet down in the recreation room. Sitting there, I saw a dozen men
with their lifejackets still on, refusing to take them off. Jimmy Counts
got up and spoke briefly about what had happened, but there was no
mention of why the rig had listed. Another American pointed out
that although they'd been having safety meetings for over a year, people still weren't sure which lifeboat to go to. Counts told him to
always go to the high side. I thought, *Yeah, sure—if you want to drop a
lifeboat down on one of those columns, go right ahead.* I don't know what
lifeboat they got in that night, which way the rig was listed, but from
seeing photos of the ones they recovered, I guess that's what the guys
did.

There was quite a bit of yelling and banter going back and forth for
about another five minutes. Finally, Counts said, "This is the largest
semi-submersible in the world. This motherfucking rig can't sink!" He
then tried calming everyone down by saying a safety inspector was
coming out in the next week to review all of our concerns.

After the meeting, I went to bed. It was eleven o'clock in the morning. I was asleep for a few hours when I was woken and told to go see
Counts. I was more than apprehensive because this guy had a real bad
reputation amongst the men. My brother-in-law had told me various
stories, one where he'd run off two brothers who'd attacked him in his
bunk. When they got in the personnel basket to be transferred to the
supply boat, Counts left them out over the ocean for the better part of
an hour. It sounded like something from the 1800s. That kind of mentality was frightening.

Counts, the captain and a few Mobil guys were there. They accused me of sounding a mayday because I had access to the radio. What had actually happened was, with the rigs so close together, I often talked to my counterpart on *Sedco 706* via VHF. I explained to them that I may have briefly mentioned the list, but I had never issued a mayday. Apparently, word had gotten back to shore of the trouble we were in—MARISAT had sent an automatic signal. Before I left, Counts told me I'd best watch out if I wanted to keep my job.

I finished out that week and left on Thursday. Before I did, Wayne, the other weather observer, asked, "Do you want to stay on and work an extra week?" I told him I'd seen enough—I was going home. He went down with the rig, as did my relief, Greg Caines.

I never worked on another semi-submersible again.

That Sunday night, the night of the storm, my brother-in-law had us down for dinner and we traded horror stories of what kind of a place it was. When we got home I set the radio alarm for seven-thirty. I woke to CBC News. They said the *Ocean Ranger* was listing badly and that the crew had taken to the lifeboats. My wife knew about the list but, I told her, we never took to the lifeboats—the report was wrong. We kept listening, and I quickly realized that this was something different, something which had happened since then. It went through me like ice.

I called my parents to tell them I was fine and got in touch with CBC. They wanted to do an interview. I was skeptical, knowing what a zoo the media was and that people always think you're in it just to get your name in the papers. But I couldn't stop thinking about the guys that were gone and how the attitude of the company men running the rig was one of total arrogance. It's the Texas oil industry—to hell with Mother Nature, to hell with everybody. To them, the crew was just peons. Marie Wadden came down and I went through with it.

When I was out on the *Ranger*, I got talking to the Port Officer stationed in St. John's. It was his responsibility to calibrate the anemometers. He came out on Wednesday and was thinking of staying. I said, "If I were you, I'd get the hell off this rig." A few years later, I was required to go to Pleasantville to do some observation testing and he was the one evaluating my performance. He recognized me and pulled out a logbook and showed me the note he'd made about our conversation. "You don't have to take the test," he informed me. "You passed."

Crane operator Bill Dugas and John Crowe. A number of crewmen were prone to calling Bill a "coonass," derided from the French *conasse*, meaning "idiot."

A MONOLOGUE ABOUT GETTING A BREAK
John Crowe; Crane Operator, ODECO

There used to be an office in Atlantic Place that hired for the offshore. The guy at the front desk said to me, "You got no experience and no trade."

"Let me talk to the rig guys," I begged him. "Let me get in there."

Finally, he said, "Be here for two o'clock."

I went back and they brought me into a boardroom with a bunch of other guys who'd all been working on the land rigs up in Alberta. Then this big Texan walked in and started interviewing everyone one by one. "You ever been on a rig?" he asked me.

"No, sir," I said. "I don't know anything about rigs. But I can work like a devil, and I can paint like a devil. Give me a crack at it and you won't be disappointed."

"We'll call you if we need you."

Before I left, I asked him, "How did you get your start?"

"Someone gave me a break."

Later that evening, I got the call. "Be ready for the chopper tomorrow morning."

I guess he saw something in me and wanted to give me a break, too.

That job was for the drill ship *Discover Seven Seas*. I was on her for six months until the *Ocean Ranger* came here.

For a while, I worked on the deck as an assistant crane operator. One time, the regular guy got sick and the toolpusher, Kent Thompson, came over to me and said, "John, you ever unload a boat?"

"Sure," I said. Of course, I hadn't—I'd only moved containers and put a bit of pipe up onto the catwalk.

"There's a boat coming in tonight," he said. "Think you can handle it?"

"No sweat."

The boat backed in and I took forty lifts off her and never so much as scratched the paint. Kent seemed happy with the job I'd done: "Soon as a position opens it's yours."

Next thing, someone up and left or quit and I was the new crane operator. That's how things used to work in the industry: you got an opportunity and you grabbed it.

Bill Dugas trained me—he ran cranes offshore for a lot of years—and the way I figure it, he must've done a decent job because I was at it for the longest time afterwards. He'd travelled most of his life on the rigs and had all the same big notions of himself that most of the other Americans had, too. I guess you could say he was the stereotypical southern oilman, true blue stamped on his forehead, and was known not to care much for Blacks or Hispanics or any kind of foreigner. I mean, he was from Louisiana, right? I got to know him pretty well, better than most guys, and learned of what a rough time he had gone through. During the Second World War, he spent a few years underground as a Japanese prisoner-of-war. I remember every time we'd have rice he'd get real pissed off because that was all they fed him during his imprisonment. There were only a few of us who knew anything about that.

All the Americans were pretty much alike. I don't know what I'd even call them. They weren't mean or nuts but they thought they were well over our heads. Bill was like that to a lot of guys. But he never did me wrong and was nothing but a nice man to work with. Jimmy Counts, however, was another breed all together. He thought he was God. Out there, they all thought they were the dominant species.

Kent Thompson, the toolpusher, had all the say aboard the *Ocean Ranger*, him and Jimmy. They did what they wanted and no one could tell them any different. If there was over fifty knots of wind the captain would phone and tell me to shut her down, it's too heavy. Then Kent would come out and want to know why in the hell the pipe wasn't up on the catwalk. If he wanted something done, that was it—there was no telling him any different. I think they got money on the side for getting holes drilled faster. If they had four months to get one done and they did it in three they'd get the big bonus. In other words, that rig had to be drilling all the time because if it wasn't it was costing ODECO money, it was costing Mobil Oil money. So if there was a problem on deck and one of my guys came to me, who was I supposed to go see—Kent? I don't think so. The next rig I went on was *Norwegian* and there was none of that foolishness.

Back then there was no such thing as a deck foreman, and roustabouts always worked for the crane operator. But I was no different than them—I never had any big position, no real authority. When the rig was drilling, the supply boat would always be around and I'd have them unload containers, or I'd keep them busy cleaning or painting. There was always something to be at. Sometimes I'd give them a break: "Do something. Just make sure it takes you a while to get it done." I always made sure to tell them to have a paintbrush in their hands, in case they saw Jimmy or Kent coming. They got pretty good at that.

When the same guys are working for days and days on end, after a few months they become a team and a tight bunch. It was only when we first went out and everyone was green that there were a few accidents. One time, coming off shift, a load of pipe was going up the catwalk and I got talking to the next crew. You never use your fingers; you always use the palms of your hands. But I was having a laugh and my fingers went in between the pipe and got caught. The guys had to use crowbars to pry them free. I broke four fingers. That was the sort of stuff new guys got into, foolish stuff that could be avoided.

I was on my time off when a guy knocked on my door. I'd never laid eyes on him before. "My name is George Augot," he said. "I'm here to see if you can get me a job offshore."

He told me he was from Harbour Breton, married to a girl from Torbay, and lived just in the road.

There wasn't much I could do for him. "George, all I am is the crane operator. I can't give you a job. But I can give you a name and someone to go see."

"No, thank you," he said. "I've got enough names. I'm after going everywhere but I can't get anyone to see me."

He started down the steps. "Hang on, hang on," I said. "I'll introduce you to the superintendent."

I brought him in and explained that he had two daughters and needed a job.

"When are you going out next?" Blondie asked.

"Tuesday."

"Take him with you."

"But I already got five roustabouts," I said.

"And now you got six."

It was as easy as that.

George was a big man and he grabbed me and threw me up into the air.

For a lot of guys who work offshore it's just a paycheque. Then you got some who want to make a life out of it. George was one of those; he loved being at sea. I'm not too sure how long he was working for me, maybe for a couple of months, when he went up on the drill floor roughnecking and then got offered a job as a shakerhand for a dollar more. I wasn't surprised one bit. He was a hard worker, wanted to learn, and people genuinely liked him.

George was supposed to come in with me that Thursday but had to stay an extra week to be trained. Before I left, I said to him, "Soon enough I'll be working for you." We both laughed.

When I found out from the radio that the rig had sunk, I spent the whole day out to the airport waiting, hoping for the choppers to bring someone in. There were a good few of us there, but no one was talking, just waiting. It was a real rough day, too, and deep down in my gut I knew they weren't going to get anyone. We all knew they were lost. I was just so numb I can't even remember how long it took for them to get on the news and make the announcement. A day, maybe two.

For the next week, I didn't know much of what was going on around me. I was in total disarray, in another world altogether—I was like a chicken with its head cut off. I remember being in the house sitting and staring at the walls, doing nothing. I couldn't figure out what was wrong with me, didn't know what was on the go. It wasn't until much later that I realized it was the shock of losing all my friends.

What I do remember is my neighbour coming over. "Get up, we're going out," he said.

"I'm not going anywhere." I was in too much of a state.

But he forced me. He knew he had to get me out of the house and around people, for my sanity.

They eventually found poor old George, and me and his buddies dug his grave over in the Torbay Cemetery. While we were down there, a guy from *Life Magazine* interviewed us and took our picture. I've still got it around somewhere. Even today when I talk about George it's hard not to cry, seeing as I'm the one that got him the job, seeing as we ended up becoming real good friends.

That broke my heart.

Jimmy Counts had the reputation of being a hard man to deal with. One American said, "The only friend Jimmy ever had was his dog. One night he came home drunk, bit the dog, and the dog up and left."

A MONOLOGUE ABOUT AN ORNERY KIND OF GUY
Larry Brazil; Wireline Operator, Schlumberger

There's been a lot of stuff said about the rig not being safe. For us, it was sometimes a month between jobs and we were often on standby, working when the rig wasn't, and we just didn't see a lot of accidents. But there were problems; everyone knew there were problems. A lot of the employees, mostly guys on the drill floor and the deck, were from the east coast, and the Americans, mainly the supervisors, weren't too happy that their buddies had to be replaced. They were all regular guys like us and once you got to know them that animosity went away. Jimmy Counts, the rig superintendant, was another story. He might've known that rig inside and out, but when he was aboard there were always crews going home for every reason under the sun. He had an awful name for himself.

Most of the Americans on board had worked with Jimmy for a long time and knew what he could be like. One of them said to me, "The only friend Jimmy ever had was his dog. One night Jimmy came home drunk, bit the dog and the dog up and left." That's what we were dealing with, an ornery kind of guy.

In transit to the well the *Ranger* was on when she sank, it got real stormy. The skipper brought her up to a survival draft and shut down the engines to ride it out. Jimmy, who went back and forth from town but happened to be on board, came on the bridge and wanted to know why we were stopped. "What's going on?" he demanded. "Get this fucking rig moving!" So they ballasted her up and towed her on.

Kent Thompson, the toolpusher, didn't get along with Jimmy much, either, and quit the rig a few short months before the rig sank. I guess they worked out their differences because he was only in St. John's two days before he came back out. There'd been something brewing between them for ages. What broke the camel's back was Jimmy said we were using too much water for washing our clothes. With him there was always something. The laundry room was right off from the recreation room, and we could hear the two of them go at it. Then Kent walked in where we were and Jimmy chased after him. They were up in each other's face shouting. Kent said, "I'm quitting." He was gone the next day. Everyone knew they didn't get along and Kent made no bones about it.

I don't know what it's like today, but back then the rig managers weren't forthcoming about a lot of stuff and had ways of getting around government regulations.

Our last winter, we were offloading fuel from one of the boats when the line busted, and oil was spilled into the water. I heard about it on the radio. In the paper, the Minister of Energy, Bill Marshall, said there was only fifty gallons spilled, just one barrel-full—that's all that was said about it. But do the math. Those hoses were six inches in diameter, pumping hundreds of gallons per minute and the rig was sixty feet up. Whatever went in the water was a lot, certainly more than what was said. The captain wanted to report the spill but Jimmy and Kent wouldn't let him. He was expected to keep his mouth shut; he was just a token. Soon after, government inspectors got involved. I can't remember if the captain quit over that or not, but I'm sure Jimmy wouldn't have been too happy about all the fuss in the media, and you can put two and two together for yourself.

The only thing that's really haunted me is the safety meeting after the list. That Saturday was beautiful—there wasn't a ripple on the water, not a ripple—and we still almost went over. It's hard to believe. There was a lot of talk that when she sank it was the operator's fault because he was green and inexperienced. But Don Rathburn, the lead guy, started off as a roustabout like him. They were looking for a ballast control operator, took him straight off the floor and trained him. He told me it wasn't rocket science: you opened and closed valves, watched the stability gauges. You just needed to put the time in and get some experience. What had happened that Saturday was the new skipper, Clarence Hauss, had relieved the operator but didn't know what to do.

We all got called into the recreation room. The safety man was there, and Jimmy walked in. He said, "You make sure to tell these men that this rig can't sink." He used much more colourful language than that, but that was the gist of it. I wasn't a mariner—that was my first time on a semi-submersible—but my thinking was that anything that could float could sink. Then again, no one challenged Jimmy because he was the rig superintendent and knew more about that rig than anyone. Who were we to question him?

31

I was out looking for the big money. I'd just gotten married and wanted to build a house. You tried to put all that stuff in the back of your mind and not think about it too much.

I was on my days off and still in bed when my wife got up to get ready for work and turned on the radio. It said a rig on the Grand Banks was in trouble. I sat straight up. The next time it came on they announced it was the *Ranger*.

I said to my wife, "They'll never get a soul off her."

It was a horrible day for weather. Nothing was plowed—I couldn't get my car out and had to take my father's—but just about all the guys were at the shop sat around listening to reports, hoping. We were pretty upset—we had good friends out there.

Someone from home went down on her, Paschal O'Neill. We went to school together. He was a roustabout, married and had a new baby. I spoke to him the day I left. He was painting the deck and I went over and he said he'd decided he was giving it up and going back to school to do a trade. Before that he'd worked at a fish plant. He was the only guy on the *Ranger* from the Southern Shore. You know what a tragedy is like for a small community: everyone's at their lowest.

Another was Joe Burry, a welder, who went out west for eleven years before coming home. Joe told me he'd been a Golden Gloves boxer but got caught up in the booze, couldn't even remember a lot of his life, and finally came to his senses in a detox centre somewhere around Edmonton. When he finally managed to get home again, he remarried his wife. I can still remember Joe telling me how good things were now that he'd straightened himself out and had his family back. God bless him, that's all he talked about.

There are lots of stories like those.

The last time they heard from the rig there was a severe list, and they were trying to get people into the lifeboats. Regardless of what he was like, Jimmy knew the rig, knew it better than anyone else. Early on, before things got out of hand, I don't think the new toolpusher, Jack Jacobsen, wanted to call him for assistance because he knew what Jimmy could be like. If he had, I don't think they would've been in any real danger of going over. I don't think I'd be talking about him and those other guys like I am now today.

Oscar Heaney on the deck of the *Ocean Ranger*. He later worked on the *John Shaw* which tapped into well Hibernia J-34 and established a flow rate, something the *Ranger* came within only a few thousand feet of completing.

HEADING TOWARDS DISASTER
Oscar Heaney; Wireline Operator, Schlumberger

t wasn't until a few years later that I learned we came pretty close to going over that morning. Once we hit a list of fifteen or eighteen degrees, or whatever it was, there would've been no turning back—she would've gone over. I've always felt that it was a warning. From where I sat, working for a service company, there was every indication leading up to it that we were heading towards disaster. Too many things... I mean, Lord Jesus, if you get a lot of incidents, eventually something is going to happen.

When six of us got picked to stay on the east coast and go out to the *Ocean Ranger*, I still didn't have a lot of experience, just one summer up in Labrador.

Things weren't much different for the guys on deck—everything was all willy-nilly and getting the operation underway as quickly as possible mattered most. As far as I could see, if you went out as a roustabout and showed a bit of interest and you were keen, before long you were up on the drill floor. Then you're around a lot heavier gear, large moving parts, and you had accidents. I saw fingers chopped off and arms broken—stuff like that. But that was no different from any rig.

When the *Ranger* came here, we were on the first chopper to ever land on her in Canadian waters. So most of us were relatively new and training just wasn't there. That's mostly where the reputation came from, why at first we might've had more accidents than the other rigs. Stories got passed around, too. Like the guy who started talking to God and jumped overboard around Christmas. Then there's the one about the rig supervisor who got the face beat off him by two brothers from Torbay. Everyone knew those. But you have to realize that although those rigs were around longer, had come from the North Sea where safety regulations were stricter, the other rigs didn't require survival suits or anything like that—they still weren't that far ahead.

Morale wasn't great to begin with. The money might've been good, but those jobs were poor. It's a hard way to make a living being away from your family for weeks on end. Entertainment was limited to a movie or ping pong. Most times you'd play cards for an hour after your shift and have a chat. There was little communication with home. You had to go in the radio room where anyone and everyone who wanted to listen to you could. What we looked forward to was eating, where everyone gathered together. The food on the *Ranger* was great, and it was hard to be out there if you were looking to lose a few pounds.

Another thing was that she had never flared—she was a virgin rig. We drilled our first hole off Cape Bonavista, but it was dry. Then we went to the southern Grand Banks. We had drilled through the Avalon Sands and were down twelve thousand feet and were getting into the Hibernia Sands, the two big oil-bearing formations out there. I remember because by that time we'd done two logging jobs. Everyone was excited—everyone—because we knew there was oil there, and it was only a matter of time before we saw it flare. That was the big talk on her.

Our fear wasn't of the rig sinking but of a blowout. None of us were trained much for the marine side of offshore drilling. The only bit of safety orientation we got was we were told where the muster station was and which lifeboat to go to. You were given a life vest to put up over your bunk, but never any more than that. The problem was we only had one lifeboat forward and one aft. Depending on the way the wind was blowing, if sour gas blew to the south you'd have to get off on the north, or vice versa. Those lifeboats were designed for fifty men, and at any given time we had eighty. We needed more. There was no way Mobil or ODECO were going to bring the rig in and stop drilling, so they shipped everything out to be installed on site: the davits, the lifeboats and a cherry picker crane.

John Wilson was the welder. Picture this: there's John in an old forty-five gallon oil drum with the neck cut out slung over the side of the rig for hours and hours welding the davits in place. That's what he was sent out in—an oil drum. I thought, *What kind of a bunch have they got running this show out here?*

Then they waited until decent conditions, brought the lifeboat around and hooked it up.

That's something else. The night the rig went down, one of the forward lifeboats was still sitting on the deck. Because the weather was so bad that winter, they never got the chance to install it.

Rig management decided to have a real drill and put a few of us in one and asked us service hands because we were sat around doing nothing. We got in the lifeboat and the motorman lowered us down and there was a loud rattling and the cables creaked. It really spooked me out. Looking around, I could see the columns of the rig and the underbelly, and I wondered if they were actually going to put us in the water because I hadn't agreed to that. Then the cables rang tight and seized. We were sitting there for I don't know how long—the motors must've tripped out or the cables weren't racked, or something—until the electricians got it going again and we were moving back up. That was a calm day and everything had been planned and they still couldn't get it right. I can't imagine how the guys did it the night she sank.

I'll always remember the captain—he went down on her. That last hitch I flew out was his first and he had the seat beside me on the chopper. He was loaded drunk and stank of booze. Who knows, I might've been stinking myself. In those days, soon as anyone came to the house on a Friday evening you broke out a bottle.

It wasn't until the morning of the list, when they called everyone into the TV room, that I saw the old skipper again. I talked to him a good bit afterwards. He'd been around the world, had been on every kind of ship, every tonnage, but never a semi-submersible. You think he would've at least had some training, but no. He was there as a paper trail and nothing more. I can't swear to this, but from what a few guys on one of the other rigs told me, there was talk the night of the storm that it got so severe they came pretty close to going over themselves but for the captain adjusted her ballast and anchors to ride it out. Thinking back, an experienced skipper might've really helped the *Ranger's* crew, too.

***

When the other two rigs were pulled into Marystown for the big inspection, everything went quiet for a few months. I ended up going on a new rig in Halifax, *John Shaw*. I wasn't too excited about the prospect of that, even if I was young and had a lot more nerve than I do now, but I pushed myself, and found a lot of the same old hands showed up on her that had been on the *Ranger*. I'm sure most of them felt the same way I did: nervous as hell.

We ended up going back out to the Grand Banks, stabbing into the well the *Ranger* had drilled, Hibernia J-34, and establishing a floor rate. I'm not sure if that was either late spring or early summer, and it could've been the next year, or the year after. But I know it was when they moved the rig because you could see the pontoons floating just above the surface, like two big submarines.

The diving company doing the wreck survey operated off our rig, and at night we'd watch the videos taped that day. On the *Ranger*, Schlumberger worked out of a tool shed located on the deck, basically a sea container. My locker was in there. I used to have this old parka, an army surplus jacket with a triangle on the arm, and I sat there one evening and watched the diver's camera go in through the door of the shed and here was my jacket right where I'd left it, now sitting on the ocean floor.

A MONOLOGUE ABOUT SOME STUFF NOT BEING TRUE
Lloyd Major; Medic and Standby Radio Operator, ODECO

I never had a problem with the Americans. You just had to know how to handle them. Before I went out, I'd heard that the supervisors called the shots. The hospital is one of the important parts on a rig—you could be dealing with a man's life—and I knew I'd have to have enough sense not to listen to outside influences. On my first day, I made it clear what was what. I said to Jimmy, "You're in charge of drilling, and I'm in charge of the hospital." We got on fine after that.

Back then there was no such thing as professional training, but I was at least a certified nursing assistant, had my first aid and for years drove an ambulance around Gander. I even worked in the Placentia hospital. On the rig, I gave out drugs, escorted patients to town and had a direct line to a doctor. There was access to helicopters, too—the whole works.

For the first few months, we had mostly green hands and a few accidents came through the doors, but nothing out of the ordinary. I'd seen a whole lot worse in the emergency room. There was a man in bed for three days because he had some wire in him that got infected. A few had their arms broke, and one had a piece of steel stuck in his eye. I'd treat them, call the doctor, explain the injury, see what he wanted done, and then give them whatever would make them comfortable while we figured out if they'd need to go in or not.

The worst was the mashed hand. It happened on the drill floor. I went in with him on the supply boat because it was too foggy for a helicopter to land. I think it was forty hours before I slept. I gave him painkillers and dressed it as best I could, but his fingers were gone. Most roughnecks got their fingers gone. If you walk down the road and see a guy with half his hand missing, you can be sure he's been on some kind of a rig. The big thing I remember was when fifty or sixty people came down with salmonella. God, that was bad. No one ate chicken afterwards, let's put it that way. It wasn't just physical injuries I had to look after, either. A lot of guys weren't used to being away from home for long stretches of time. They'd get lonely and depressed and would want to call their wives or go in out of it. There wasn't much I could do for them besides try to get their spirits up.

The Americans knew the oil business, but that's common sense and stupid to think any different. It was their rig and they'd been on it for years before they came up here. But a lot of Newfoundlanders didn't like being told how it was going to be. It didn't help matters that Jimmy'd fire two or three guys just about every shift. If you were standing around doing nothing you'd be gone. Some guys would get off the chopper and if he didn't like the looks of them they'd be sent right back home again. I was out there the night the two brothers from Torbay beat the piss out of him. At two in the morning, he phoned me from his room. When I walked in, he was in some state: his eyes were black and his hand was cut. Another time, John Crowe came in from the deck—I was in the hospital—and tore the doors off Jimmy's office and put his fists up in his face. I don't know what it was all about, but I tell you one thing, that was the first time I ever saw Jimmy back off from any man.

One time, the two of us went up on the drill floor to do an inspection. Ralph Melendy was smoking; Jimmy didn't see it, but I did. I went over to him. "Ralph, if he sees you, you're shagged." He took the cigarette and doused it in his hand and had to come down later to get it bandaged up.

To his credit, if Jimmy'd been on her the night she sank, she never would have gone over. That's a fact. First thing he would've done is fire everyone.

The hospital was right across from the Mobil and ODECO offices, and whenever I went over to tell Jimmy this one or that one was off work because he was sick, there was never any bullshit. I was straight and forward. At first, they had me out there as a Medic 1 so they wouldn't have to pay me as much as they should've been. Ed Norwood was the superintendent over Blondie, had a dozen rigs, and was the hardest kind of old skank if there ever was one. Him and Blondie came out one time and caught a bad bout of the flu. They wanted me to give them something. "No, sir," I said. "There's drugs in St. John's, but they're staying there. Make me a Medic 2 and they'll come out tomorrow." That's all there was to it.

You just had to know how to handle them.

A few guys were bitter about the way they got treated because some of the stuff that's been said isn't true. Safety drills were held each week, and everyone was taken down to the lifeboat and taught how to get in and strap themselves down. Everyone was told this, meeting after meeting, down in the television room. Chairs were lined up and we all had to sit down and sign the sheet stating we'd attended, and then the safety guy would get up and give a talk for an hour. I was out there when the rig had that list, too, and everyone was at their lifeboat station with their lifejackets on. A few people ended up at the wrong lifeboat station because it'd been made clear to us that if the rig was listing to the bow everyone was to go to the aft, and if she was listing to the aft everyone was to go to the bow. Always keep to the high side.

It was still pretty scary when I could stand in the radio room and look out over the port crane and see the horizon.

When my ex-wife turned on the radio the Monday after I got off, I said, "That rig's either afloat or sunk."

With the *Ranger* there was no in between. She was so big and had rode out so many waves—the biggest I ever saw was fifty-four feet, which broke over the helideck—but the waves that night were a hundred feet. Don Rathburn was out there for that one. I thought we were safe as a church when he was in control, and if he couldn't keep her trim no one could.

I called the office, got ready and went down to Pier 17. I knew everyone on the rig. It had been my responsibility to allocate rooms when the guys got off the chopper, me and the safety man. You're living like a family out there; you know them, everything about their lives. I did the tentative IDs for ODECO and then blacked them off of the crew list as if they'd never been there to begin with. The experience was about what you'd expect it would be. You got all kinds of company men down there, understandably upset, and they're with you in the waiting room, you're all in the room, and I'd say something like this one is from your company and then they'd go in. I always recommended they not do that, I recommended they not see the bodies for themselves.

The first time was the hardest. It was Ken Blackmore, my relief. I went down to the morgue and did the positive ID because his wife was in Norris Arm. I wanted to take him home, and there ended up being an awful racket over that. Blondie said, "You're not going anywhere."

I stopped in my tracks. I certainly wasn't putting up with the likes of that. "You don't tell me anything. You're talking to the wrong lad, my son. I'm going to Norris Arm and you can go straight to hell!"

The head honcho of ODECO was there, the President, never mind Blondie, and he came out and said, "Lloyd can go wherever he wants. You see to it he has a car, a hotel and a good set of clothes. Park his vehicle in our garage and gas it up."

Jimmy and I went out with Ken's personal belongings, his last cheque in my back pocket. I went in and introduced myself to his wife and three children. It was the longest living room I've ever walked across. Her family asked me to sit up in the front of the church with her. But I just couldn't—it didn't feel right. It could've been me on the rig instead of Ken; in fact, we had even talked about changing shifts.

It was something I didn't want to have to go through, identifying bodies. But I stayed strong to get the guys home and laid to rest.

When the rig sank, everyone was like, you got to do this, this and this. Follow procedure. ODECO figured iron out the problems later and do whatever extra needed getting done now. They did their damnedest; I don't care what's been said since. I saw that with my own two eyes. It's not like I'm just saying this now, it's not like I was all buddy-buddy with them, or something. I had a lot of good friends go down on her, Newfoundlanders.

MEMORIES THAT WILL LAST FOREVER,
BUT WHICH WILL MAKE ME SAD FOREVER
Wanda Frampton; Bartender, The Chalet Lodge

The Chalet Lodge used to be just off the Trans-Canada Highway. It's gone now—it burnt down years ago. Before that, it was the Old Fort, which is what some people still call it.

I started bartending there in May 1981. I was eighteen but told them I was nineteen because it was either that or work cash at a supermarket. For the first six or eight weeks, I was doing great. Then they told me I had to go get a liquor license. *I'm busted now,* I thought. Jim Toussaint, the owner, asked me to go pick up his wife's license and a few others, and because I had a swarm of them I just asked for mine and got it. It was as easy as that.

The Chalet was the happening spot for guys in the oil industry. The four years I spent there were pretty crazy times.

The companies had it arranged so that guys working on the rigs who lived out of town would stay there while they waited to head out. We used to pick them up at the airport, take them back to the Chalet, and when it was time for them to catch the chopper, drive them to the heliport. Other times, if the weather got too bad, they'd be there for an extra week. That was the regular thing.

I guess I knew every guy who ever stayed there.

They used to call them "rig pigs." Some of them were all about flashing money and were pretty obnoxious about it, too. That's where the nickname came from.

William Dugas was definitely a "rig pig." He always had this gold chain around his neck with his initials in diamonds, and he wore a blue polyester leisure suit with a fat belt buckled at the waist. It always reminded me of Mr. Furley on *Three's Company*—he was just like him. He used to tell a story about being in a posh New York hotel and hitting on this woman who happened to have a poodle in her arms. She wasn't going along with any of it. He looked at her and told her kindly that animals weren't allowed in the hotel. But it was her pet, she explained. "I was talking to the dog," he said. That was typical William Dugas for you.

Most of the guys were sweeties. Ken Blackmore was someone I always remembered. He was constantly going back and forth between Norris

Arm and St. John's. All he ever talked about was his family—he was totally devoted to them. Porta Test had a party, a function, and I was bartending. Greg Tiller and a bunch of them were all sat around the table drinking and laughing for hours. He had such a big smile.

I knew Derrick Holden from Mount Pearl—he lived off of Topsail Road, right next to where I went to school. I used to play hooky with Derrick's two brothers and he'd pick us up in his Trans Am—that was his baby. God, he drove like a maniac, and I always thought he'd be killed in a car crash. He was cracked. Derrick happened to be up to the Chalet, and the guys said he'd drink anything, absolutely anything, and they dared him to down a dishwater and rum. It was the nastiest drink I ever served, and I couldn't believe he swallowed it. He was a bit of a case, a ticket, but he was a doll, too, an absolute doll.

It's been so long since I've thought of them that there's a whole whack whose names I can't remember. But I can still see their faces so clearly. They were all a good laugh.

Some of the guys waiting for a ride home would want me to cut their hair or trim their moustache to look good for their wives and girl-friends. I didn't have a clue what I was at, and their moustaches would always be way up here or way down there or they'd be near scalped on one side of their head. They didn't care—it was all good. Then there were the safety awards they'd win like *Ocean Ranger* T-shirts. We'd try them on and they'd say that with pontoons like those the rig would never sink. Some of them would ask you to write them a letter, and we'd send them a piece of paper in an envelope with an "A" written on it, or box up little floaters for their arms in case they wanted to jump overboard, or a bag of marbles in case they lost their marbles. Like I said—a good laugh.

With the wages they were earning they were always the best tippers. I was getting $2.85 an hour and there were a lot of times when I could bank my paycheque and live off tips. They'd always flash money around. A few guys took six or seven of us down to the Fishing Admiral and ordered a couple of bottles of Don Perignon to drink with our meal. Another time a guy was picking up flowers for his wife. "How come I never got flowers?" I asked him. He came back with two dozen yellow roses.

Some of them became my drinking buddies, too.

If they lived in St. John's, they probably had an apartment between three or four of them. The companies had houses they'd rent to their employees because it was cheaper than having them stay in a hotel for a month. Most of them were party houses.

We were young and wild. We never had a clue what was about to happen.

I was on my way to work when I heard the rig was listing. When I got in, a whole bunch of people from ODECO, Schlumberger and Halliburton were sat around waiting for word, all eyes and ears turned to the television and radio.

There was a rumour going around that Jimmy Counts had been out on the rig. We weren't sure if he was actually on it or if he'd just gone out, if he'd even made it through the storm. In my naïvety, I figured that if Jimmy'd been out there some of the crew must've made it back with him.

Then he walked in with some Search and Rescue pilots, and I ran up to him and started pounding on his chest. "Tell me you were on the rig! Tell me you were on the rig!"

He couldn't answer me.

Then I knew they were gone.

We spent the next day waiting to see if they'd find the lifeboat, hoping there'd be someone in it, praying that at least one person would be found alive to make this thing okay, someone who could say what the hell had happened out there.

Reporters got wind of us having a two-way radio to the rig, heard rumours we'd been talking back and forth with them throughout the evening, and they started crawling around everywhere. None of it was true. There was this one guy from the States who was just so insistent—I couldn't tell you what paper he worked for—but he had to know word for word what we'd said to the rig and who we were talking to. There was no convincing him otherwise. We would've given anything to have had the chance to talk to them one last time, anything—I told him that.

Friday was the longest day. A crowd of us met up at the Chalet and made our way to the service at the Basilica. When I walked in through the doors, I was completely overwhelmed by the number of people that'd turned out. There wasn't even enough room for everyone—

people were standing anywhere they could find a spot. Me, I was like a zombie, just numb with sadness, and this gentleman, I had no idea who he was, still don't, had never met him before in my life, came up to me and put his arms around me. "I know, my darling—I know. My son was out there, too." It still hurts to think about him.

For years and years, I was consumed by it all. I used to go up to Cape Spear and Signal Hill and sit in my car and cry for hours, thinking about how frantic their last minutes had to be, how absolutely terrifying it must've been for them wondering whether or not they were going to make it. Losing that many friends, I nearly cracked up—I nearly lost my mind. I mean guys like Carl Fry, being at a party with them and thinking they were just so cool and then waking up one day and poof they're all gone.

After a few years, I had to let go.

I made a lot of friends who worked on that rig, and to be able to think about them again is pretty great.

I have many memories that will last forever, but which will make me sad forever.

THE 85ᵗʰ MAN

Gary Wall; Wireline Operator, Schlumberger

I went out that week to fill in for one of their regular guys and was supposed to crew change on Monday morning. Although you got assigned to one rig, the company would often move you around—it wasn't unusual at all—and at that point I'd already been on the *Ranger* about a half dozen times.

Those seven days were pretty uneventful. We'd go out in the morning and do our work, come in for dinner and coffee, finish up whatever needed getting done, and then come back in for supper. Like I said, uneventful. There was nothing ever unusual about the *Ranger*, at least not that I can remember. It was no more dangerous than any other rig I was on, and I was on every one out there then. On the other hand, my usual rig, *Zapata Ugland*, was a pig. She was dirty and small—a scow. But you trusted the crew, the Norwegians. They were seamen and they knew what they were doing. When I first got on her, they showed me the lifeboat, started the motor and made sure I knew what to do in case of an emergency. The attitude on the *Ranger* was a whole different story. The Americans were arrogant, often drilled too long, and thought she was unsinkable. But she was real nice and pretty damn stable, and I don't know but it's a bunch of bologna that she was unsafe. I'm a very safety-conscious person, always have been and always will be. If I felt she wasn't safe I'd have said something or wouldn't have gone out in the first place. It's as simple as that.

Saturday morning, I received a Telex from the office saying I'd had a house fire, and there was a number to call, my neighbour's. Sure enough, we'd had a fire, but there was only a bit of smoke damage—nothing serious. They just wanted to let me know in case I phoned home and there was no answer.

I spoke to the company man about going in. Normally they'd accommodate you if something tragic had happened, but this was Saturday morning and no flights had been booked, and there was no way they were going to bring out a chopper when no one belonged to me had died.

That night, a bunch of us were watching a movie starring that guy from *MASH*. I liked his movies, but for some reason got bored and went upstairs. Walking up the hallway, I heard the chopper's call letters.

"There's a chopper on the way?" I asked the night radio man.

"Yeah."

"Where's it going?" I thought he said *Sedco 706*, that she was stuck in the hole.

I went back to the company man. "Remember our discussion? There's a chopper headed towards the next rig."

"All right," he said. "Get them to come over."

By the time they circled back, I had my bags packed, was waiting just inside the doors and got talking to Albert Howell. He was trying to quit smoking and just to be a devil I gave him the last pack of cigarettes I had on me.

The chopper made a pass but couldn't land; the rig was titled just a bit. They tried again and managed to set her down.

As I was going out the door, Perry Morrison passed by. "Take me in the bag with you," he said.

"Get in," I laughed.

As we flew off, I saw the lifeboat which lay on the deck waiting to be installed, the reflection of the moon on the water. When I close my eyes, I can still see those things so clearly.

We left the rig around quarter to twelve. It wasn't a windy night, probably twenty or thirty kilometres an hour, just a breeze, but enough to let you know it was there. When we landed in St. John's an hour later there was blowing snow and gathering banks of drift. It'd become one miserable old night.

The guy who checked in my suit drove me out to meet my wife. We stayed at her mother's.

The morning I was supposed to crew change, my brother-in-law was taking an early flight back to Devry University in Mississauga and most everyone in the house was up. I was on a cot in the living room and Debbie came and shook me awake. "What rig were you on last night?"

"The *Ocean Ranger*. Why?" I asked.

"It sank."

I didn't think it was one bit funny.

"I'm not joking," she said.

When she turned on the television the reports indicated they'd lost radio contact at 1:30 a.m., just twenty-five hours after I'd left for town. Man, my jaw could've hit the coffee table.

One of my best buddies, Rick Haley—we'd gone out to Edmonton together in the late-70s—was on *Sedco 706* that night and for three days couldn't get in, wasn't allowed to make a phone call with everything tied up. He thought I was dead. Soon after, he quit the offshore because his son was having nightmares, went to work up in Ontario and was run down by a car and killed. We used to call him Dusty.

The night I got in, I called my boss and told him. He wasn't too pleased. But when I arrived at the office on Monday, he put his arms around me and said, "Jesus, it's good to see you."

A guy from CBC came by my house begging me on his knees for an interview. I had nothing to say, couldn't talk about the rig's stability or the operation because that hadn't been my job. A lot more people had a lot more knowledge than I did, which wasn't too much to begin with.

The important thing was I had my life. Everything else was inconsequential.

I got the "Why me?" syndrome. I thought, *Why wasn't I out there? How come I was so lucky and no one else was?* It certainly affected how I felt inside and how I dealt with people. Sometimes it was hard to keep my composure, and I went through a long period where, for instance, if someone cut me off on the road I'd curse them down and shake my fists at them. I'd often get upset at work, too. Around six years ago, I got some help and came to terms with what had happened as best I could. It was something I had to do.

Even after twenty-seven years, I thank God every day for being alive. If I die tomorrow, get struck by lightning or drop over dead with a heart attack, I have to be thankful because I've had twenty-seven more years than those other guys got. Looking back, I wish Perry and all the rest of them could've gotten in that bag and on the chopper with me, too.

The starboard side of the *Ocean Ranger*. It was porthole #4 which shattered under pressure from a massive rogue wave, setting into motion the tragic chain of events which ultimately sank the rig.

SWEARING: A POSTSCRIPT
Frank Dyke; Radio Operator, ODECO

The Royal Commission said that the glass porthole in the ballast control room was smashed by a wave. For three years, I watched the action of the seas, wrote down what I saw in my logbook, and not once did a wave hit that starboard column hard enough to shatter four inches of glass. I'll swear to that until my dying day.

All around the underbelly of the rig there were hoses for pumping oil and drill water. They had huge brass and copper fittings. I bet you one of those hit that porthole.

The week the rig sank, I was answering some questions up to VOCM when this guy from ABC, Ted Koppel, called. "I understand you were the radio operator and have a logbook. What's in it?"

"Everything that had to do with the operation of the rig," I explained.

"Would you sell it?"

Out of curiosity, I asked him how much he'd pay.

"What about fifty dollars?"

"Not tonight, Mr. Koppel," I said and hung up the phone.

Soon after, Leonard Martin, chief counsel for the Royal Commission, contacted me and said I'd be a prime witness. Two staff sergeants from the RCMP interviewed me, then two lawyers, and they said the same thing. I was never called.

Two or three guys I knew from the *Ranger* stopped talking to me and refused to take my calls. I thought, *This is strange*. Mr. Martin and the two Mounties wouldn't talk to me, either. I went to the hearings and told them who I was and that I wanted to testify. But they simply weren't interested.

I was in Venezuela on another rig when Canada Oil and Gas Lands Administration phoned my wife wanting to know when I'd be home. I paid them a visit and spoke to a deputy minister. "You're going to be our man in St. John's, Frank."

The following Friday, I went back to get the details and was informed they'd rescinded their offer.

Senator Jack Marshall was a friend of mine. I told him what was going on. "Forget about it," he said. He wouldn't say why.

I couldn't figure out what was going on.

My neighbour was with the National Research Council in Ottawa. I told him my theory about the hoses. "They just don't want to believe what you're saying," he said. "They've already made up their minds and they're frightened to death of what you have to say."

A wave could never have been hard enough to break that four-inch thick glass. Never, never, never. Those hoses busted that porthole, caused water to get in on the control panel and short circuit it. That was the company's fault—it was a design flaw, just like how she couldn't recover from a severe list. I'll swear to that on my mother's grave. I'll swear, I'll swear, I'll swear.

PART 2

THE CASUALTY

It seemed I saw a claw of the living wind
tear grey hair from the haggard sea's sad jaw,
the air—a flayed and fraying fabric
flecked in white—
mad banner of the earth's despair.
It seemed I saw
the maw of the living world
and the death of water.
— David L. Benson, "Jogging: Tail of the Bank"

Mother Earth created us, raised us,
taught us, sheltered us, and this
is how we repay her.
Beware, she shall have her revenge.
— Greg Tiller, "Rig"

A little oil costs a lot of blood.
— John McGrath, *The Cheviot, the Stag*
and the Black, Black Oil

Gordon Windsor was aboard *Sedco 706* when the *Ranger* sank and two of his brothers, Robert and Steven, lost their lives. The following morning he was airlifted to St. John's.

A MONOLOGUE ABOUT STARING OUT OVER THE RAIL
Mike Cole; Motorman, Sedco 706

After dinner, I went on watch in the engine room, did my rounds and took my readings. I was writing in my log when the rig jolted once or twice. Because of the storm, all the engines were going and running hot, so we had the garage doors open a bit. Suddenly, water just poured in. I was startled and jumped up. There was a life jacket station where I worked, and the first thing I did was throw one on and pull the flood drains. I thought there was something wrong, something serious, but then the sea water started to go down.

I called up to the control room. They said a hundred-foot wave had hit us, which was about the equivalent to four feet of water on the helideck.

A few guys went out and checked everything. There was some superficial damage: a mounted life raft was gone, steel railing was snapped, some containers had broken loose, and our high beams beneath the rig were bent. But even with one of the anchor winches having lost tension, there wasn't any real cause for concern.

We heard through the grapevine that the wave had hit the *Ocean Ranger,* too, and she was experiencing difficulties: a smashed porthole and stability problems. There was confidence it would be resolved because any issues we'd ever had were. Jack Jacobsen may have called over—I'm not quite sure. He'd been our night company man before heading over to the *Ranger,* and everyone knew him fairly well. The plan, just to be safe, was to transfer all of their nonessential guys over to our rig, and a few of us got the recreation room ready with whatever extra blankets and pillows we could find.

One of the things that really sticks out in my mind are the helicopter suits. Not everyone had one in their cabin; there were just fourteen or so up on the helideck for the crew changeover. I took one and stashed it away. Before the night was out, they were all gone.

I was up listening by the radio room when the plan got cancelled— the *Ranger*'s crew seemed to be doing all right. In emergency situations, the radio room was off limits, but the operator was a nice guy and would give us updates on what was going on.

Some time around one, Jack called over to inform us that whatever problems they were having couldn't be resolved. Then, half an hour later, another message: they were leaving the rig and wanted us to relay a mayday. That's the last we heard from them.

The drill floor was shut down and no one was allowed up on the deck, and some of us were sat around in the coffee room and the locker room talking amongst ourselves about what was going on over there, some saying they knew this one or that one, a few very concerned because they had family aboard that particular rig.

One of them was Gordon Windsor, our derrickman. I didn't know Gord prior to my life offshore. We met on *Sedco 706* and became good friends. He was a quiet guy and reserved, but really easygoing and someone who you wanted to get to know. I just can't remember ever hearing him curse, which was pretty uncommon for a place with a bunch of men bunked up together and no women around. For a lot of us, we'd be off for a good drunk as soon as we got in, but Gord wasn't like that. He was a family man and would rather be out in the woods with his brothers hunting or salmon fishing. His brother Roger worked out there with us on the opposite shift. They were a lot alike: real good guys.

Where he didn't drink much, when we found out he was getting married, we put off a little thing for him, figuring he might not be up for a bachelor party. Me and his buddies were joking he'd soon be tied down for good, and we wrestled him to the ground and cuffed a ball and chain to his ankle. Everyone got a kick out of it. That's a good memory.

Earlier that Sunday, we had disconnected and brought our rig to survival draft of fifty or fifty-five feet, which gave us more freedom to ride the waves. In late December or early January, we got hit by a massive wave in a pretty heavy storm. The rig rolled a good bit but there was never the feeling that something horrible would ever happen. No one took that stuff too seriously. I mean, we were leaning out over the handrails looking at the waves. Then again, for some reason, the *Ranger* was going over—it just as easily could've been us.

Gord wasn't on duty, couldn't sleep, and was hanging around with a bunch of us. Everything was shut down, and we were sat around talking. Most of what was said was fairly positive, but in my own mind,

57

and I'm sure it was in Gord's, too, was the deep fear that along with his two brothers, the *Ranger*'s crew were lost. But no one ever said it. The main thing you got to remember is there was always the hope, despite what was going on.

As time passed, more rumours: a lifeboat had come up alongside a supply vessel, men were in the water.

Then, at around 3:30 a.m., the blip that was the *Ranger* disappeared off the radar. No one knew what to think. Gord had far more at stake than any of the rest of us, but somehow managed to keep his emotions to himself.

Early that morning, just after dawn, our company chopper came out to refuel—it was still windy as hell, maybe seventy knots, and the guys manning the helideck had to tie themselves down so the gusts wouldn't take them—and we heard them say life jackets had been spotted, but there were no signs of anyone. Management arranged for Gord to leave the rig. I wasn't up there but was told he had to hold the netting just to walk out and get aboard. Even then we figured there were people out there somewhere waiting to get rescued.

The supply boats came up not too long after, and the company told us that anyone who wanted to go in could, and to come back only when they were ready. I think the talk that the rig had sunk, and not just drifted off location, scared people. Eight guys, nervous about staying out any longer, quit. All but one of them ended up returning. A friend who went in asked if I was leaving, too. I couldn't. "If I go in now, I won't come back, ever. I think I'll stay where I'm at."

As the weather cleared, we found out for ourselves what had happened. *Sedco 706* was just eight miles from the *Ocean Ranger*—you could see it. It's a pretty empty feeling looking out over the handrails and the rig is gone and you know eighty-four guys are gone with it, including Gord's two brothers, Robert and Stephen.

A MONOLOGUE ABOUT THE DRILL
CONTINUALLY TURNING RIGHT
Rick Flynn; Radio Operator, Mobil Oil Canada

There were several of us banging around town, all ex-military, who applied for jobs through Harvey Offshore Services, when I got a call that they were looking for a radio operator. There wasn't much work available which fit my credentials and, not wanting to go away again, I started off with ESSO's drilling program in April 1979.

We had an office on Torbay Road, but towards the end of that year the company's operations—one here and one in the Davis Strait—began to wind down. They turned everything, lock, stock and barrel, over to Mobil: the rigs, the personnel, the whole nine yards.

Shortly thereafter, they moved us down to Atlantic Place.

For the most part, the job was uneventful. Rigs and drillships had come and gone, as well as supply vessels and helicopters, without incident. You might get the odd medevac or severe weather warning, some quasi-emergency situation where we'd assist in relaying for Coast Guard or Universal Helicopters, but there was never anything critical. It was a well-oiled machine.

Although that night was particularly stormy, it was no different than any other, and I started my shift with weather forecasts.

At one o'clock, we received an alert from the *Ocean Ranger* that they were listing badly but attempting to isolate the problem.

A few minutes later, the night radio operator requested a mayday. I called Coast Guard, notified our onshore supervisor, Merv Graham, who was at home and in communication with the rig via MARISAT, and within the next thirty minutes people started arriving at the office and the heliport.

In terms of drilling and logistics, there was a level of professionalism you'd come to expect from your colleagues and yourself, but no one was prepared to respond to such a situation in that kind of storm. Isolated in the radio room on the seventh floor of Atlantic Place, I couldn't fully appreciate its severity until I received word a Sikorsy helicopter, pulled from the Torbay hanger, was blown straight across the tarmac.

It was still very early on when ODECO's rig superintendent, Jimmy Counts, showed up. Standing next to me with his supervisor in New Orleans on the line, he said, "I'm flying out to save that rig." I thought, *Don't you mean you're going out to save those boys, those men?* For me, it was a telling example of the indifferent attitude of the industry. It cost $100,000 a day to keep the rig going, and it was common to charter a plane just to fly in a five dollar screw from the US. For them, human life seemed insignificant to the drill continually turning right.

Soon after their original message, the *Ranger*'s radio operator informed me they were taking to the lifeboats, and I relayed another mayday. That was the last we heard from them.

Our people started to arrive en masse and a communication post was set up for faxing and telexing. With our helicopters en route and Search and Rescue being mobilized out of Gander and Halifax, there was still a sense of confidence: *We're going to make it. These guys are going to be okay.*

An hour later, the *Ranger*'s stand-by vessel, *Seaforth Highlander*, radioed that they were within visual proximity of a lifeboat, that they had seen a flare and were going to try and get closer. Merv Graham was in the room and had me relay to them not to put a line on it. He had heard of an incident in the Gulf of Mexico where a lifeboat had capsized while being towed. I later learned that as men started to emerge and gather along the gunwale, Graham's worst fears were realized and all the men were thrown into the water.

In the office, it was as if it was the middle of the day—everyone was mobilized, the phones were going mad, the radio crackling steadily—and then at three-thirty in the morning *Sedco 706* radioed that the rig had disappeared off their radar.

We then knew things weren't going to turn out good, and a sense of finality and resignation seemed to subdue everyone, a pervasive feeling of helplessness. We had all of those resources but could do nothing. I wondered, *Is there anyone even left to save?*

The main thing going through my mind was my friend, Greg. He was the day radio operator and out on the rig that night—it was only his second hitch. We had worked together at the Mobil office for years. He was young and engaged, and he and his girlfriend—who had filled a hope chest with those things that young married couples need—would often come over to the house for dinner and a beer. Even after they'd abandoned the rig, I couldn't help but think he'd have one helluva story to tell for years to come.

Sometime late that night, his mother called me. I'd never met her, only spoke to her the few times I'd phoned to wake Greg to come in for his shift because he had a real problem getting out of bed. How could I possibly tell her he might not come home?

There were other guys I talked to over the radio who worked for the service companies, guys I knew by name, but couldn't put a face to. In the old days, you could recognize someone from the tap of their Morse code—it was like that.

Everyone knew someone out there.

Maybe that's why no one wanted to state the obvious: *The rig is gone and there are no survivors.*

I once toyed with the idea of working on the rigs. Although there was much made of it afterwards, I never thought of the *Ocean Ranger* as an unsafe rig. But from the guys I met, you got the impression the company was too focused on the business at hand. *We're going to do this our way, no matter the risks.* Thankfully, with a baby at home, I decided against it.

That morning, I left the office and didn't return for several days.

Steve Romanski, the Mobil area manager, was crucified by the media because of our woefully inadequate response. We had taken off and landed in some pretty bad weather, but nothing like that night, and we were unsure of what to do. The companies were so caught up with getting oil out of the ground that they didn't give any thought to things going wrong, like the rig capsizing, because land rigs don't capsize, and that's where they had all come from.

I was fairly young then, in my early twenties, and couldn't comprehend the impact of that kind of negligence, particularly on the young women, the wives and girlfriends. Now, with a family of my own, I've often wondered if Greg's fiancée moved on. What became of the dreams they shared? And the hope chest? I never did speak to her again, didn't know how.

A MONOLOGUE ABOUT NOT BELIEVING
Jerry Higdon; Second Mate, Seaforth Highlander

I was working for Harvey's on the *Bonaventure II*, did a seventy-day hitch and was on leave for a month, when I got a call from Seaforth Maritime wanting to know if I'd be interested in going second mate on a supply boat, the *Commander*. I was between runs—at that time, it was ten days from St. John's to Montreal and back—and continued on until January when the *Highlander* came over, and I was told to go to work on the south side of the harbour.

Until she heard it on the radio, my wife didn't even know I was out in the oilfield. As far as she knew, the ship had sailed to Halifax with a load of casing. We were supposed to make just one trip out to the rigs but got stuck with standby duty for the *Ocean Ranger*.

The week or so I spent on the *Seaforth Highlander* was a horrible time.

I remember busting my leg real bad while unloading cargo to *Zapata Ugland*. A forty-five gallon barrel of oil had broken loose and was going back and forth across the deck. It wasn't so dangerous when we were in close to the rig—we put it back and left it there with the intention of securing it when we got out—but when the skipper pulled away, the deck slick with grease, I slipped, the barrel rolled, and I got pinned into the edge of the warping drum. When she rolled again, I managed to haul myself free. Sick to my stomach with the pain, I got the gear off and saw that my leg was black. Blood was pooling under the skin, streams of it running down to my ankle.

I was on watch and said to the old man, "You best have a look at this."

He asked if I wanted to go up to the *Ranger* and see the medic.

I said no and bandaged it up as best I could. That was a lifesaver.

The next day the weather came up and got really bad—the bottom had fallen right out of the barometer—and the wind was good enough that even with our head into it we got pushed further and further from the rig. There were times she'd pound so hard I thought we were going to come apart. Even with the four engines running over seven thousand horsepower, the ship would still fall off on one end. I wouldn't be able to guess how high the waves were. I've been out in sixty-odd foot seas and those were a joke compared to that night. One minute you're looking down into the trough and all you can see in front of you is a wall of water, and the next you're looking up at the sky overhead.

Because of my bad leg, the skipper and I split the watch.

It was around one o'clock when we got a call from the *Ocean Ranger*. They asked us to come in closer to their buoy pattern. They didn't say why, either that or I can't remember, and there was no sign of them being nervous or anxious, or anything like that.

Five minutes later, they called again. This time it was an emergency, and I handed it to the skipper: "We're listing to the port. All counter-measures are ineffective."

I've heard stories over the years that there were all kinds of stuff going on long before they called us. But we weren't notified of any porthole breaking. If they had notified us, we would've been better prepared, would've taken more risks.

With the skipper shoving on the sticks, we fought to get there.

I kept trying to reach the rig on VHF but there was no answer. In my gut I knew no one was there and that they'd gone to the lifeboats. It was scary thinking about the luck they'd need to survive.

We had no life-saving equipment. The boat had just arrived from the UK and had never been used in a standby role. The mate, a long-time mariner, went below. He got a gangway net and rigged up a makeshift scramble net, put some lines on it so it could be weighed down and stretched over the side for men to grab hold to. There were fifty-foot painters, a few boathooks. It wasn't much.

Just before we got to where the rig was supposed to be, I saw lights through the snow and a flare went up off our starboard bow. As we made our way towards it, I saw another.

That's when we came upon the lifeboat. There was a large crack in the bow of her and she was taking on water. The press later reported we'd run her down, but I'm sure that hole was there before I ever laid eyes on her.

The skipper tried to line her up and get her astern. It was unreal to watch. If he hadn't known our vessel we would've been a statistic ourselves.

A hatch in the lifeboat opened and someone emerged. The mate and four seamen—I couldn't see who— threw a life ring with a rope attached. The guy caught it and tied it to the railing of the lifeboat. The next thing, seven or eight of them came out and stood along the gunwale. Then the lifeboat just tipped over and they were all thrown in the water.

The mate told me later he reached out and almost had one guy—he got that close.

Years ago, a lobster boat left Port au Choix for Lark Harbour but never showed up. I was on the ship that came across her, bottom up, a body tangled in rope down around the props. When they brought him aboard, I helped lift him onto a stretcher and his foot rubbed against my arm. I can almost feel the goose bumps, even now. Vivid things like that stick with you. I imagine almost getting that guy from the *Ranger* stuck with the mate, too.

The men could barely stand and it took everything they had just to hold on. One of them ran forward and released our life raft by cutting the rope, the spray having frozen it. It landed right among the guys but no one grabbed for it. With the water temperature as low as it was they were just too weak to help themselves. If they could've got in it they might've lived.

I saw all this from the bridge.

The skipper had me go below and haul on a bit of gear to see if I could help. By the time I got on deck, there were no signs of life, and men were drifting face down in the water.

None of us could believe something like that could actually happen.

The next day was the worst. Steaming up to where the rig was supposed to be, bodies and life jackets were floating all around us. Whoever was in them must've gone unconscious and slipped right out. I can still see one of their faces, like he was looking at me and no one else. We saw just one with a survival suit. The rest weren't dressed in any amount of clothing. They were in a real hurry to leave the rig— it wasn't a well-planned abandonment.

Even as the search widened, there was still hope for survivors. Search and Rescue directed us towards a life raft, and the crew was all hyped up and excited that someone might actually be found alive. We were flat out getting ready. We found it capsized, the canopy all shredded. We then discovered it was our own, that we had launched it, and the bottom dropped right out of us.

We were out for another full week.

Shore wanted us to come in to find out exactly what we had seen. The skipper refused. It had been our rig and we wanted to stay with the search. But the ship required a new fuel purifier, and all we had were a few filters. We had other problems, too. There was a crack in the cover belonging to the steering controller—hydraulic fluid had leaked all over the floor—and a light was gone on the rudder indicator.

"We don't know how long we can keep her going," I said to the skipper. "If we break down, we're in trouble."

We contacted Coast Guard and set course for town.

I felt a little useless then, and I'm sure the rest of the crew were the same way. It's something I've carried with me. Over and over and over again it goes through your mind that there was more you could've done. But I know, for what we had available to us, and there wasn't much, we did everything humanly possible to save those guys.

Taken from the deck of the supply vessel *Boltentor*, which was on standby for *Sedco 706*. On the night of the loss, seas were reported to be sixty-five feet and winds one hundred knots.

A MONOLOGUE ABOUT WHERE
WE WERE AND WHERE WE'RE AT NOW
Thomas Kane; Deckhand, Boltentor

Back in the late-70s, I worked for Shimo Shipping running containers from St. John's to Montreal. Offered the opportunity to work offshore, I spent the next few years on various vessels doing supply and anchor work. Towards the middle of 1980, I ended up on the *Boltentor.*

For the four years I was on her, she had a good crew of twelve men and an experienced English skipper.

When the *Ocean Ranger* first arrived on the Grand Banks, we put her on location, and then for the next year ran cargo and fuel to her, stuff to keep her going, and sometimes did personnel transfers when it got too foggy for the choppers to land.

That morning was nice, but as the day wore on the winds picked up and the skipper and first mate warned us a storm was brewing and to close the watertight doors and batten down the cargo—it was going to get nasty.

I was doing the eight to twelve watch, and when I first came on it was already blowing seventy-five knots. But we were comfortable—those old supply vessels were good sea boats.

On standby for *Sedco 706,* they radioed to inform us waves were breaking over them but they were doing fine. The skipper then took us upwind so that if anything should happen we could get on-site quickly.

At quarter after twelve, I went below and crawled in the bunk.

An hour later, my relief said the *Ranger* had put out a mayday. Thinking there wasn't much to it, I lay back down. Not long after, our rig gave us clearance to head over to see what could be done, and the old man got everyone up.

For Newfoundland, even in the North Sea where they'd been at it for some time, safety appliances and Search and Rescue was a whole new ball game. But whatever we had we got ready: tugging wire for our safety belts, boathooks, ropes and life rings.

The skipper came on over the radio: "We should be seeing the *Ranger* soon."

A rig in the dark is lit up like Christmas. I was on the portside with the watchman and saw just three or four lights in the distance. Then several containers floated by.

Coming up on the rig's starboard quarter, there was a break in the storm and it was clearly visible that waves were washing up over the helideck.

We circled but found nothing—no survivors, no lifeboats.

All that day the seas had come in slow and built with the growing wind. I was out late last year and they were seventy feet. Off the coast of Nova Scotia, we had the windows on the bridge beat in by a sixty-foot wave. The night the *Ranger* sank was something else altogether. That night, at its roughest, the waves were clocked at eighty foot, the winds a hundred knots.

Other supply vessels had proceeded to the area. The *Seaforth Highlander* radioed they had a capsized lifeboat and men in the water and wanted us to assist.

I saw those men.

In the pitch of darkness, the water-activated lights of the life jackets were like stars in the night sky.

We went for them—that's all we had to go by. There might've been thirty of them. Four of us were on deck, one man watching the seas. It was like a seesaw in a vast valley of black. With the waves swelling forty feet over our heads, as soon as you got alongside someone down in the trough he'd be gone again, the crest breaking and coming down and taking you up the other side. We saw one man in his overalls, his hand breaking the water, his life jacket blinking. Our boathooks were twelve foot, but we could never get close enough, never had enough rope. I couldn't say if he was alive or dead—I just couldn't tell. With the wind blowing and the snow spraying, I was amazed we got a chance at all.

Soon the wind had blown the lights away and spread them out over a mile. The skipper would steam towards the few he saw, but the weather was such that there was nothing we could do.

Then the *Nordertor* radioed: "Where's the *Ranger*? We don't have her on radar."

We went to her location, where she was supposed to be, but there was nothing.

We steamed back to *Sedco 706*, hung around and turned in.

The next morning we woke to the news of what we already knew: the *Ranger* had sunk.

What started out as a rescue effort became a salvage operation. We teamed up with the *Sir Humphrey Gilbert*, zigzagging a mile apart, spotting for bodies and debris.

On the seventh day, continuing on alone, we found a lifeboat. Submerged, the bow was barely sticking out of the water. A few of the guys jumped on top and hooked a cable so we could haul it aboard. Before we did, the skipper had us look inside for men. But it was filled with water and there was no way to tell. When we got it on deck we realized there'd been nothing. And it was beat to shit: the stern was smashed as if it'd been released with no one in it, or pounded by containers or pipe, the enclosure flattened. The sea could've done an equal amount of damage.

Thirty-four miles from where the *Ranger* sank, we located a life jacket, steamed up to get it with the boathooks, and realized a body was attached. We wrapped a wire around him and hoisted him up onto the deck with the crane. The skipper wanted to know if he had any identification on him and had us go through his pockets. We found a wallet. Because the seas were still rough, he couldn't be left on deck. The skipper said, "He's someone's father or son, of course. And, no offence to the man, but we don't know how long we're going to be out here. We don't want the elements getting at him." Wrapping him in blankets, we put him below deck.

For us, being seamen, the worst was seeing what the water could do to a man after just a week. It wasn't a nice sight; not a nice sight. A few of the boys quit over that.

We continued on for some time, but found nothing.

Pier 17 had been cordoned off by the RNC—that's where we docked. An ambulance was parked, and the attendants came aboard and got the body. A crane hoisted off the lifeboat and the bit of debris we'd recovered. For the next few days, officials from the Department of Transportation, RCMP and Coast Guard, as well as the Provincial Government, sat us all down trying to figure out just what had happened, when all we wanted to do was to get back to our families.

I testified at the inquiries in Boston and St. John's. Among other things, they wanted to know if we could've done more to save those men. I don't think so, at least not with the gear we had and in those conditions. Even now, with over thirty years at sea, and after all the changes and improvements that have come since the *Ranger* sank— FRCs, immersion suits, man-hooks, bigger boats—I still don't think we could've done much. We saw those guys in their shorts, jeans and over-hauls.

Photo courtesy of *The Telegram*

The remains of the *Ranger*'s #3 lifeboat being unloaded at Pier 17. Stowed on the deck and waiting to be installed, when it was picked up by the *Nordertor*, it contained no fuel or provisions and the seat belts were still rolled up.

A MONOLOGUE ABOUT FEELING BLOODY USELESS
Patrick Fahey; Second Mate, Nordertor

I was the second mate on the *Nordertor,* a German-owned vessel contracted by Crosbie Offshore to do supply and anchor work for *Zapata Ugland,* about twenty miles from the *Ocean Ranger,* our crew Canadian, but mostly Newfoundlanders.

The second mate's watch was from midnight until four in the morning, and then from noon until four. That particular night, we were on standby a short distance from the rig, dodging back and forth at about three knots. I was in the wheelhouse; a watchman was up with me. He was in the after part of the bridge when he burst in. "Mate, did you hear that? There's a mayday over on the *Ocean Ranger.*" I hadn't heard a thing, but he was certain. Then it came on again, and I had him wake the captain.

As soon as the captain got on deck, I said, "She's in real trouble. We've got to head over right away."

Before I could even spin the ship around, we received a grim message: the crew was abandoning the rig. An icy feeling came over me then, one of dread. I didn't know how many guys were on that rig, but I knew there were a lot. *Jesus,* I thought, *this isn't good. This is a disaster!*

I've gone to sea for the better part of thirty years, and I have never experienced a rougher night than that. When we jogged and turned we rolled pretty good, but when we opened up the vessel and gave it to her, things really got going. One wave came straight over us and smashed the binnacle clean off, ripped up the screws and bolts and the plate holding it in place. The whole thing came off and left us with a hole on the top of the wheelhouse. Water came down and shorted out our automatic pilot.

We were getting so much sea clutter on the radar that I could barely make anything out. But I could see the rig as well as a second target, the *Seaforth Highlander.* At about the same time as the captain asked me if I still had her on screen, she vanished.

There was a lot of radio talk, messages from shore to watch out for lifeboats, and I had our guys go out onto the catwalk along the bow to spot for survivors. I was on the searchlight. None of them could hang on, and they tied themselves to the rail with one-inch manila rope. As we got closer, we started to come upon sparkles in the water. The realization then hit us that those were life jackets and men floating just below the surface—dead.

We wanted so desperately to get them out of the water, regardless of whether or not they were gone. Your biggest fear going to sea is that you'll be left behind. There's nothing like the feeling of bobbing up and down and losing sight of your rescue craft, the mother ship. A few months later, Crosbie Offshore was the first to implement the German-designed Fast Rescue Craft. They had us jump off the ship in the roughest kind of weather with one guy left to rescue us, endless miles of water all around. I could only imagine what it was like in the early hours of the morning and in those conditions wondering if you were going to make it. The boys tried their best to get boathooks on them, but the waves would yank them right out of their hands. I was spared a lot of it, assisting the captain and spotting for waves, but everyone was soaking wet and freezing and feeling so bloody useless. We couldn't even get near many of them—the sea was too rough. When I was called before the inquiry, the judge asked, "If it was so bad that night, how could you turn around and come back for those men? It must've been dangerous." I explained to him that it was our job, that we couldn't just leave them without trying. He couldn't understand that.

A lifeboat came close to the ship. It had a life ring attached and a hole in the bow. We had a line around the props, and the skipper tried to take it over the stern, but it rolled at the wrong time and we had to cut the engines. The chief mate was there and said he could see right down into it and that there were a dozen or more men still strapped in their seats. Eight or nine spilled out through the hole, but they were already gone. A wave came, the stern went down and one of them washed right up over the quarterdeck and hung over the railing. The crew ran back and hauled him up. All he had on was a jean jacket and one boot—he wasn't wearing a lifejacket. We brought him up to the winchhouse and covered him with a sheet.

Later, I spoke to some of the crew about what it must've been like for the *Seaforth Highlander*, thinking you were going to save those men in the lifeboat—such a feeling of hope, and then disaster. We never even got that chance.

That same day, *Sedco 706* directed us towards a lifeboat. We used to lasso the buoys at the end of a rig anchor with steel cable and haul them in. The boys decided it was the only way to get it. I knew what steel cable was going to do to the fibreglass hull and went back to the bridge and expressed my concerns to the mate. "That's not going to work," I said. "It's going to crack." Sure enough, it cut off the canopy and got crushed when we took it over the back deck. No one was inside.

We radioed in and they told us to start for shore, other ships were headed to the scene. Ordered to maintain radio silence, some of the guys were worried about their families. We called the office. Phyllis, the secretary, said, "I'll get in touch with all your wives and tell them you're not in any danger." That helped ease our minds.

We had been up for thirty hours trying our best, unable to stop for nothing. Everyone needed rest, especially the poor captain—he had been through so much. He told me later that he was so exhausted that when he finally got to bed it was like falling into a tunnel.

On the way to port, the sea spray was bad. Every time we took a dip, water came up over us and froze solid. We got out with wooden mallets to beat the ice off, but we just couldn't get ahead of it. By the time we reached St. John's, we were listing over thirty degrees. It was a scary situation for all of us.

We docked on the south side of the harbour and RCMP investigators came aboard. They took out our logbook and started asking questions about what the entries meant. We were so tired and they kept asking the same questions over and over again. It didn't make any sense. Here we were, having gone through this traumatic event, this tragedy, and they wanted exact times and scenes laid out in detail. It was mind-boggling, crazy.

It affected everyone differently. The captain went deeply religious. Spared the worst of it, I wasn't haunted. Until I saw the crewmen's faces on the news and read their names in the papers, they were just voices over the radio.

It has since become a memory, part of my life at sea.

Bob Sonntag and his daughter, Erin. Bob died suddenly in November 1984 while preparing to take over command of helicopter operations at CFB Cold Lake.

THE DARKNESS OF A LITTLE HOUSE
Cris Sonntag; Wife of now-deceased
Search and Rescue Pilot, Bob Sonntag

Nothing makes my heart race and stomach burn like the sound of the phone ringing in the raw hours of the morning. It's one of the lasting effects of being married to a Search and Rescue pilot—a gentle form of battle fatigue.

The phone was on my side of the bed, and it was me who picked it up when bad news came bellowing into our bedroom. I handed the receiver to Bob at about half past one on that Valentine's Day and heard the name *Ocean Ranger* for the very first time.

As I listened to the one-sided conversation, always terse, always brief in military-pilot jargon, I heard the words "lifeboats" and "listing." I looked to the snow-covered window and heard the sound of the storm battering wet bullets against the house, and my stomach lurched with empathetic queasiness for the poor souls stuck out there.

Pulling the covers up around my face, I was confident there would be no way the choppers would be going out. An image of a Newfoundland ferry flashed into my brain. We had been in Nova Scotia for something to do with Bob's job and had taken our two children, Matthew—an infant—and Erin—eight—to see their grandparents. Upon our return we had boarded the midnight ferry in Sydney and gone straight to our cabin to get the children settled. We were due to arrive in Port Aux Basques sometime in the early morning. When I opened my eyes around six o'clock and we still hadn't left Sydney Pier, I knew we were in for a very long ride.

Every time I think about that crossing, the slob ice banging and assaulting us, the screaming wind and angry seas, I think about the *Ranger* and what the men faced that night. Until you've seen the great North Atlantic in those kinds of conditions, you can never truly understand what bravery in the face of adversity on the high seas means.

I stood in the cold kitchen and did my usual duties of watching him eat and reminding him to be careful. For some reason, Bob wouldn't talk. There was something he didn't want me to know. It was only after pulling the information from him that I realized what was really going on.

"I'm waiting for the Mounties. They're going around picking up the two crews in a jeep. They're the only ones that can get through this—they have a plow on the truck."

I looked out into the storm. The snow was coming down sideways, so thick it was hard to see the neighbour's house across the street. Even the stop signs, already barely poking out of the drifts from the last storm, were hardly visible.

"You're kidding, right? They're not getting the choppers up in this?"

Silence was his reply. I could feel fear beginning to take hold of both of us as we sat and stared out at the storm.

The phone rang again. It was the Mounties. They'd be picking Bob up in five minutes. End of discussion.

We waited in silence until an eerie red light flashed into the storm and drew close to the house. Bob grabbed his knapsack and rushed to the door. Before he stepped into the storm, he turned his face to me and we were in each other's arms. "I'll call when I know something."

Then he was gone.

I don't remember returning back to bed. All I could do was wait in the dark and listen while outside the nor'easter roared on and on, piling up the snow and covering the tracks of the vehicle that had just taken away my husband. I was sure whenever the decision was made I would get a phone call.

I remember feeling horribly alone and wondering who else on this Godforsaken rock knew about what was happening out there. The families of the rig workers would know by now. They would be awakening to news that their loved ones were in danger while the rest of Newfoundland lay sleeping. Perhaps invisible lines of support were inching their way from house to house. Priests, ministers and family members would be calling. Teapots would be warming on stoves, cups rattling. I learned of the power of the Newfoundland teapot not long after I arrived. Throughout every generation of Newfoundland women, it's always on the stove ready to soothe and comfort in times of crisis.

Then it hit me as hard as the snow slamming against my living room window. *What about me? What about how I feel right now? Who is going to call me up with promises and words of reassurance?* In the darkness of my little house on Byrd Avenue, I got down on my knees and prayed to

God that if and when my husband and his crew donned their gear and climbed up into their aircraft, He would go with them.

I had never really worried about Bob before in all his years as a pilot, never really let myself think about the dangers associated with his job. A dark thought flashed through my mind: *What would my life be if he was lost to us?* I couldn't imagine myself as a single mother.

Later that morning, I heard the unmistakable thrum of two helicopters. I knew what that meant. They had waited until the weather abated and the winds died down. The snow had stopped, leaving us buried under the worst storm Newfoundland had seen in decades. School was cancelled and nothing was moving, not even the snowplows had made it to the side streets. I still had not received a call.

The television was to become my source of information. All day long, local and national news were broadcasting the disaster. It wasn't looking good. The rig was gone and aircraft from St. John's had been sent out to search the water for lifeboats. They brought back only bad news. Radio dispatches from another rig, as well as a ship in the area, were being played over and over. The Labradors from Gander had left St. John's and were out flying over treacherously high seas in horrendous conditions. I couldn't believe they had actually sent them out.

The day passed before I could get any news from anyone in the squadron, and it was only to say that no one had heard anything from the pilots and probably wouldn't for quite a while. Between shovelling and running back in to check on my children, I would sit for a few minutes, eyes and ears glued to the television, hoping for a peek at the horizon for any aircraft returning safely to land.

It wouldn't be until late the next evening before I looked up and saw the face of Mike Clarke, the other pilot aboard Bob's flight, talking to a reporter with CBC. Mike's expression was strained as he searched for the right words. He looked exhausted as he spoke into the camera. He told of attempting to lower a SAR tech towards the water to a potential rescue, only to have a mighty wave sweep the victim away from his arms. Apparently, the brave technician wanted to stay down and try again, but it was becoming too great a risk with the waves swelling to a height well above the blades of the helicopter.

Walking around the aircraft were three figures. It was easy to pick out my husband. His tall figure towered over the other two. He was carrying a knapsack and had his head lowered into the wind. I was to learn afterwards how he had managed to avoid the reporters that plagued the crew as they left their aircraft. After nearly nine hours of holding a helicopter in the air over waves nine stories high, fighting against gale-force winds pummelling the aircraft with icy spray that threatened to bring it down into the Atlantic, it was hard for him to find any words of false hope and comfort.

A week would go by before I heard my husband's voice. An inquiry was to be held, and both helicopters would be sent back out over the water with press and government officials. Bob's conversations with me were short and to the point. He could not talk about the rescue to me or anyone else, and I hated the not-knowing.

I knew my husband was frustrated by the bureaucracy of it all. No one was allowed to leave under any circumstances until someone gave them the clear. But nobody seemed to care what these men had been through or how desperately their own families missed them and just wanted them home and safe.

It would be at least two weeks before the crews were released and returned to Gander.

Finally, when he could, Bob had a very hard time talking to me about what it was like out there. He spoke of the attempt by the SAR tech to recover the body from the icy waters, his eyes tearing up, and he would tell me again and again about the courage it must have taken for the young man to volunteer to go down into that hell.

"If you could have seen what we lowered him into… We had to order him back up or we all would've died."

He talked about refuelling in those stormy seas and how the aircraft couldn't land on another rig's deck but had to remain in a hover while fuel was pumped by crew chained to the platform. So they weren't engulfed and dragged into the frigid North Atlantic, he held the aircraft's nose steady and his eyes on the swell of the gigantic waves, rising and falling with them. He described seeing overturned lifeboats and orange life rings bobbing around empty. As one member of his crew put it, "There was nothing moving out there except seagulls."

Photo courtesy of Wayde Butler

The *Sir Humphrey Gilbert* was diverted to the *Mekhanik Tarasov*, a distressed Russian cargo vessel one hundred and twenty miles east of the *Ocean Ranger*. It eventually sank with the loss of thirty-two crewmen. There were only five survivors.

THE WORST WEEK OF MY LIFE
Wayde Butler; Quartermaster, Sir Humphrey Gilbert

Sometimes I would talk about it and other times not, because seeing a dozen bodies lined up in front of you is too hard for some people to grasp. We came out of it alright, never suffered any casualties or damage, no one was hurt, but it was an awful situation and a horrible experience. It was the worst week of my life.

By February, I'd been working on the *Sir Humphrey Gilbert* a few months as a quartermaster, which included steering the vessel and doing security watches. Involved in a lot of hard cases and vicious storms, she was a mainstay in the Coast Guard's fleet. She was multi-purpose: an icebreaker, a cargo carrier and good for Search and Rescue.

I was on leave for the weekend, had gone with my girlfriend to visit her parents in Adam's Cove, and even then, on Friday, the weather was miserable. By next morning, the jeep was buried. I wasn't supposed to work until Sunday night, but because the radio was calling for the "big storm" we headed back to town.

The forecast wasn't far off: it was the dirtiest of nights.

It was around two in the morning or maybe three or four—I'm not too good on times—when several supply vessels left the harbour. I thought, *Something strange is going on.* My relief, an old seaman who was prone to telling tall tales, came in at seven-thirty that morning and said an oil rig had tipped over. I had been up all night, was tired and wanted to go home, and simply wasn't interested in what he had to say.

Later that morning, my mother woke me. "The ship is calling. You've got to get back to work right away."

With everything ready to go, we left the harbour just before noon.

While in-transit, the news came in over CBC: a rig *had* capsized and it wasn't in the Gulf of Mexico or anywhere else, it was here.

Our chief officer started asking boatmen if there were any cod jiggers on board. At first, I couldn't figure out what they wanted them for, but as soon as he mentioned filing the barbs off the hooks the reality of the situation began to sink in: we'd use them to retrieve bodies from the water. That was about the extent of our preparation.

Back in those days, our means of communication was limited to St. John's Coast Guard Radio and Morse code. There were no satellite phones; I'm not sure if even the offshore had them. We picked up a message that we were to divert our course towards the *Mekhanik Tarasov*—a Russian cargo freighter located one hundred and twenty miles east of the *Ocean Ranger*. She had declared a mayday shortly after the *Ranger* went down but cancelled it, then six or eight hours later declared another.

By the time we arrived, Tuesday or Wednesday afternoon, the *Mekhanik Tarasov* had sunk. There were two vessels on the scene, a Russian factory ship and a Danish trawler, *Sigurfari*, which had been Johnny-on-the-spot and recovered thirteen bodies and five survivors. They transferred them to us.

The sea was still pretty rough and there was no way for us to get alongside the other boat. We took a rocket-line, shot it across, connected a ten-foot Zodiac and shuttled it back and forth. It was the only way. We took the five survivors first. I pitied those poor men for having to get off the trawler and into a little rubber Zodiac after what they'd already gone through. With the *Sir Humphrey Gilbert* and the *Sigurfari* heaving in and out only feet apart, I was surprised they weren't crushed. The men were in remarkably good shape considering they survived by lashing themselves together into a huddle. They didn't say much, spoke very little English, but the one who could was relatively calm and responsive. The youngest had these wild eyes and bushy hair, like what he'd seen had cracked something within him.

We took bodies four at a time. It was really strange to see them all out on deck. I was up in the wheelhouse for the worst of it—dragging them up over the railing, wrapping them—but it was still shocking. We had nothing—no body bags—and wrapped them in bed sheets and put them in the helicopter hanger. It was obvious the crew had been caught off guard, like they'd gotten out of the bunk and jumped overboard, because a lot of them were in their underwear and T-shirts.

It wasn't until months later, when an insurance company contacted the skipper, that we got wind of what was thought to have happened. A ventilator was beat off in the rough weather and sea water got down into the cargo hold, which contained newsprint. As it got wet and swelled, it increased their list until she rolled. It seemed to me that when the end finally did come it was quick.

Wednesday night got really bad. The Rescue Coordination Centre in Halifax wanted us to stay over and do search patterns in the event someone was left out in a life raft. That surprised me. You would think that with survivors on board they would want us back as fast as we could get there. They must've figured there was hope for finding others.

I was on the wheel and the anemometer clocked winds gusting at ninety-five knots. A wave came in over the stern and washed right down into the crew's deck. We had guys so terrified they sat up in the mess the whole night with their life jackets on. Even the seasoned veterans found it hard. If a rig as big as two football fields and a two hundred and seventy foot long cargo ship could sink, something one quarter the size of that surely didn't hold out much hope. For them, that was their last trip to sea. I'm surprised more didn't quit.

I was no different than those guys, and some things that bothered me stuck. Part of my duties was to make the rounds every hour. One of the stations was in the helicopter hangar. With the howling wind, driving snow, the boat pitching and tossing, I told the first mate I couldn't go in there, just couldn't. The other quartermaster had more guts than I did and went in instead. Even now, on stormy nights, I have trouble sleeping. Radio broadcasts were continuous: mayday relays, updates, reported positions of debris. A two-tone auto alarm indicates a distress message. Even though I ended up in marine communications working distress situations, two-tone auto still gives me the creeps and makes the hair on the back of my neck stand up.

Sometime Thursday, we headed back to St. John's, arrived early Friday, and were met outside the narrows by a small wooden naval reserve vessel which brought us body bags. We tied up at Pier 17. Several Mounties came aboard with Customs and Immigration, as well as an official from the Russian embassy, took photographs and removed the bodies. The survivors got hustled away.

All of us had gone on some case and picked up someone lost in an open boat or a longliner that sank, and you got two or three survivors or a body. Even now with seventy-five footers, you're talking about five or six guys. This was something else. There were no debriefs—no nothing—and for days I had this terrible knot in my stomach. Forty-eight hours later, it was still there. One of the senior managers said, "What's wrong with you? They're dead. Suck it up and get on with it."

I stayed with Coast Guard, got my certification as a watchkeeping mate and finished off as a chief officer. Having spent a lot of time on Search and Rescue vessels, I was involved in other incidents, including mapping the debris patterns of the Air India disaster. If stress is accumulative, then those things have coloured me, stuck with me, and my mind often brings me back to that week.

A converted supply ship, the seismic vessel *Java Seal* eventually recovered thirteen of twenty-two bodies.

A MONOLOGUE ABOUT LOOKING AND
LOOKING AND LOOKING
Carl Staubitzer; Motorman, Java Seal

I don't have a monopoly on the sea, haven't spent fifty years out there like some guys, but I've seen it so rough that I never thought it would ever calm down again. Anyone who says it's not the hardest place in the world to make a living doesn't know what they're talking about. My uncle was a merchant marine during the Second World War, and he told me there were many guys who resigned the Navy and went to the front lines in Europe rather than face another trip across the North Atlantic. It's amazing just how savage it can get.

That February was no different. It was a real poor winter to be out there.

It'd been a decent day and we tried to get some work done—as a seismic vessel sailing for Geophysical Services, we mapped the Grand Banks, found the Hibernia site and most of the natural gas deposits off the coast of Labrador—but having lost cable in early December because of rough weather, once the sea started to swell, we hauled in.

By ten o'clock, it was blowing a pretty good gale.

Sometime after midnight, we were playing cards and watching a movie, and the skipper called down from the wheelhouse that we had a mayday, a rig was in trouble. There was a meeting in the galley and someone suggested we gather up whatever gaffs and lifebuoys we had lying around. Our life rings, which were fifteen pounds, were no good because you couldn't throw them against the wind—we needed something beefy. There was a lot of chain and roundstock aboard, and we made up grapplings with rings and floats at the ends—something for the men to grab hold to. With that sort of stuff you might hit them in the head or cut them in the arm or the body, but at least you had a chance to get them aboard.

None of us had any proper Search and Rescue training and certainly weren't prepared for that type of operation. All we could do was pull together and draw on whatever experience we had.

The skipper knew what we were about to face. "Don't take any unnecessary risks. We already got a tragedy and we're not going to lose anyone else. There's to be no pictures of bodies coming up over the side of the boat, either. I don't want families looking at snaps of their loved ones splattered all over the newspapers."

When you're out in those kinds of seas, you definitely go the extra mile to save someone. But when it's a recovery situation you have to keep in mind that it's only a body you're after. You're safe and dry on the boat and there's not much sense in two people losing their lives. I know I'd want it that way if it was me in the water.

That's all you can expect from someone.

I lost some good buddies on the *Arctic Explorer*, guys I had gone to school with. One minute they were in the galley cooking eggs and the next floating down the coast off St. Anthony in two inflatable life rafts. That was the middle of summer, in calm seas, and thirteen of them still never made it. In the conditions we faced that night, there was a grim chance of survivors, a grim chance. As soon as anyone hit the water that'd be it for them, they'd be finished.

We were only twenty miles from the *Ranger*, but because the weather was so rough we couldn't make any headway. On the radar, it'd show us a half knot ahead, a wave would come and crash down over the wheelhouse, and we'd go half a knot astern. But the skipper couldn't drive her any faster or we'd be sunk ourselves.

When we got there in the early hours of February 15, all hands were on deck. It was pitch black and driving rain and none of us could see a thing. It was 50/50, but we made a judgement call and turned on the searchlights. They kill your field of vision any farther from their reach, but if we left them off we'd surely miss someone. If they were in a lifeboat, at least they'd see us through the sleet and put up a flare. We looked all that night with lights on and lights off, but found nothing. There wasn't a soul out there.

The next morning there was a lot of chatter coming in over the radio about the *Seaforth Highlander*, and everyone, including us, was searching in the area where the lifeboat was thought to have drifted.

Two of us spent three days up on our helideck just looking. The others were up in the wheelhouse and on the wing of the bridge, everywhere. Just looking and looking and looking.

On that first day, we found four. Only one was dressed in an immersion suit with an inflatable collar, the rest in jeans and a shirt and a small red Pilly Pugh life jacket. That's how we found them, their life jackets floating and their body hanging just below the waterline. To one guy, they looked like roses.

I couldn't understand that part of it, what they were wearing. At least they could've put on a heavy coat or wrap themselves in something, anything, plastic bags and duct tape if they had to. Unless you were the radio operator, the last guy off the rig, how could you jump off with just a shirt on? Things must've gone bad pretty quick.

The next day, just before dawn, I saw a flock of seagulls off in the distance, circling. My uncle told me years ago that if you're looking for things on the water, look for gulls. Because we were supposed to start searching in another zone, I booted it up to the wheelhouse. "Skipper, I think we got something."

Jesus... We found ten boys. Right there. And a lifeboat.

They were all floating in that same area.

The sea was still a bit rough, and the skipper manoeuvred the boat so that when we drifted down on top of them the water smoothed out a bit. But it rolled at the wrong time and they went under. We lost two; eight resurfaced. Because we were a converted supply vessel and our back deck was only three or four feet from the water, we could hook a gaff into their clothing and haul them up over the side.

The cook wanted us to put them in the cooler, but some weren't having it. The decision was made to lay them up where we kept our Zodiacs and to cover them with a tarp. There was mention that we should look through their pockets for identification. I was dead set against that for fear something might get mislaid or lost, like a memento or a wedding ring.

One of the crew wanted us to take the lifeboat aboard, too. All we had was a little cherry picker which could only handle three tons. The lifeboat certainly didn't weigh that, but bottom-up and filled with water, it was more than we could possibly handle. Sure enough, the cable busted.

The skipper radioed the *Nordetor* and we stood by until they had it up.

We got the last body on my twenty-fourth birthday. That's how I remember it.

Shortly thereafter, we headed back to shore.

We arrived just outside of St. John's around three in the afternoon. The photographers had a field day when the *Hudson* docked, and we were told to wait until night. Under the cover of darkness, we unloaded the thirteen bodies.

A few nights after we got in, the company threw us a big party up at the Battery Hotel. They had a full spread on and gave everyone some kind of pocket knife. The saying aboard the boat was "Do or die for GSI!" That's the Texas mentality for you: *We dodged another bullet, boys.* That kind of old stuff.

I didn't feel much like partying and stayed home. It could've just as easily been me drowned in the water.

THE DEPTHS OF THE RIG
Max Ruelokke; General Manager, Hydrospace Marine Limited

I t was an exceptionally stable rig, and the only one I ever worked on that had a pool table. Seldom would the cue ball ever wander off. When we were setting up the initial diving system, I spent several months out there. After supper, I'd walk laps around the perimeter. On one particularly miserable night, with the supply vessels bobbing up and down, I thought, *I'm glad I'm here and not out there.* Maybe that's why I never worried about my crew's safety.

Hydrospace Marine Services started life as Underwater Visual Systems, owned and operated by Bill Ludeman and I. We were in the business of providing underwater TVs. I was a young engineer working for the Federal Government and Bill a former diver with the Royal Canadian Navy. After talking with some guys who'd come out of the US Navy and had gone on to have fairly successful careers in the private sector, we decided to change the name and expand into commercial diving.

In the late fall or early winter of 1980, we won a contract to provide our services for Mobil Oil Canada aboard the *Ocean Ranger.*

We had a five-man crew, four divers and a supervisor, which did close to sixty dives, mostly observation and routine mechanical tasks, our system consisting of a bell and a decompression chamber. At the bottom, a hatch would open—the pressure on the inside would keep the water out, the other guy breathing normally—and the diver would exit the bell. At the end of the dive, they'd head back, close the hatch, come up, and the guys on top would have hot coffee and sandwiches waiting for them in the decompression chamber, while the supervisor gradually lowered the pressure.

Because they weren't as busy as the rest of the crew, they tended to help out if extra hands were needed. It was a close-knit bunch.

My memories of that night and the following day are still vivid.

I lived in Mount Pearl with my wife and two kids. We had a kind of tradition to go to Swiss Chalet every Sunday, but that evening was too stormy. I said I'd go anyway to grab some takeout, pulled on my ski-doo-suit, jumped in our old Land Cruiser and crawled up the rough trail that was Walton's Mountain.

In moderately rough weather you hoped they weren't diving—that's when it could get dangerous. But this was such a bad storm that I knew they weren't working. They never crossed my mind.

At quarter to four in the morning, my phone rang, and I awoke like a shot. It was a drilling engineer from Mobil—we knew one another quite well.

Christ, there's been a dive and they had an accident. It flashed through my mind. I quickly dismissed that; there was no way they were out.

Before he had a chance to say it, I somehow knew.

"We think we've lost the rig," he told me. "Get your personnel files and come down. Everyone needs to start notifying the families."

I called Bill and met him at Atlantic Place. Five of our guys were out there, and we split them up—I called three and Bill two. The rig had disappeared from the radar, we'd lost visual contact, so all we could tell the families was that we thought it might've sunk, but that Search and Rescue had sighted lifeboats. There wasn't much else we could say other than as soon as we heard anything we'd call. There was a lot of hope that first day, but I knew, instinctively, that the outcome would be grim.

It was tough. Norm Halliday had been an only child in a single-parent household. I could really relate to that—my mom had raised me on her own—and I knew how strong the bond could be between a mother and son. It tore my guts out to phone her.

Nobody knew if the rig had sunk on location or if she'd drifted off twenty miles. The *Balder Cabot*, sailing out of Halifax, was deployed to come down and find out. It arrived in St. John's on February 16. The only underwater mobile intervention system that existed on the east coast were Mantises, one-man submersibles with manipulator arms and thrusters. Having worked off the *Balder Cabot* for years, we already had them in place. Someone was needed to make on-the-spot decisions, and it was decided that I should go and manage the operation.

We left the next day and searched until the end of the month.

The seas were rough, preventing us from getting in the water. But with several of the anchor buoys still left, we were able to determine the centre of the rig's mooring pattern. The possibility existed that the *Ranger* had sunk straight down in two hundred and sixty feet of water, the derrick just breaking the surface, and we proceeded cautiously.

I went to check the echo sounder. The sea floor was flat, our equipment showing nothing but a straight line, and all of a sudden the indicator shot straight up to about one hundred and thirty feet. We knew it was the rig, capsized approximately five hundred feet southeast of the wellhead.

When the weather cleared, we deployed a Mantis and kept divers in the water twenty-four hours a day. Over a period of two weeks, we did a gradual survey of the rig.

Everyone speculated, including me, that bodies might've gotten trapped on deck or drowned and sank to the bottom. Although we were vigilant in our search, we never found any evidence to suggest that, and no one was found.

Very early on, during the first few days, Mobil management thought it possible some of the crew might've sought refuge in the depths of the rig. I don't know if Merv Graham, Mobil's onshore supervisor, and Jack Jacobsen, the toolpusher, had conversations about it or not, but Merv was adamant that Jack might have done that. "I just have this feeling," he told me.

There was a small void space next to the pump room. It was possible they could've survived there for some time.

We tried signalling them by banging against the pontoons. No one banged back.

Mobil asked that if we heard someone, if there was a noise, could we do something. We had a hastily contrived plan which would've seen us burning a hole and getting a diver in there with an oxygen mask. At those depths and working within that timeline, it would've been extremely difficult. But not impossible.

We gave up when it became apparent that even if someone had gone down there they would've succumbed to hypothermia. I never believed anyone would've done that; it would've taken a special kind of person.

Over the years, I've been asked why my crew hadn't put on a dry suit—the equivalent of a survival suit—or gone down into the diving bell which could've been pressurized and cut loose. I think they all made a decision. None of the rig's crew had any marine qualifications, had never worked in that sort of environment, and basic survival training was not a requirement. My guys all had experience working from marine platforms. We'll never know if it's true or not, but I'm sure they were pitching in and trying to help everyone else. Saving themselves would've meant abandoning their shipmates. Gary Crawford was with the company for quite a while. He was the sort of guy to make sure everyone got off first and would've worried about himself last.

Everyone on the diving team agreed there was a need to find some kind of closure. When we were in for fuel and supplies, I had one of our guys hike up to a flower shop and get the biggest kind of wreath he could find. I said to the captain, "When Mobil tells us to come back in we'd like to hold a service, for ourselves." I got together a bible, a hymn book, and typed up an order of service.

At midnight, we shut down the ship, put her on dynamic positioning right over the centre of the rig and went through the ceremony. There wasn't a dry eye on board.

At the end, we tossed the wreath off the stern, stood there and watched it drift away.

Everyone kept that very quiet. I'm not sure if it's even been mentioned in public.

By the time we got back, the Royal Commission had been established. We knew there was going to be a significant survey required and were determined to get the contract. Having lost five guys, five good friends, we wanted to be there. And we were, with most of our time spent at the third starboard column. Even then there was the thought that whatever problem had sunk the rig may have begun there. We were the ones to cut out the porthole, remove the ballast control panel and bring them to the surface.

We put a bid in for the salvage operation but were turned down. A Dutch company won that contract. I called them up: "We were the diving contractor for two years and know the rig intimately—we did the survey. I've got experienced divers I could put at your behest." They chose not to do that. Three of their men were killed that first week.

PART 3

DAY OF RECKONING

In St. John's, business had come to a stop, but sidewalks and streetcars were jammed with people all hurrying to the cable office on Water Street. The news had spread through the town by word of mouth: "Another Greenland disaster."
— Cassie Brown, *Death on the Ice: The Great Newfoundland Sealing Disaster of 1914*

The darkness of sorrow covers our beloved province.
— From Archbishop Alphonsus Penny's opening sentences at the ecumenical memorial service, February 19, 1982

TWO MONOLOGUES ABOUT BEING YOUNG
Part I: Barbara Yaffe; Reporter, CBC News: The National

Towards the end of 1981, I was posted to St. John's as national reporter for CBC News, having completed quickie television training in Toronto. Getting a chance with *The National* was a big deal for a young woman from a somewhat sheltered background who up until then had only known print journalism. This was all adventure with a capital "A."

Only weeks before the *Ocean Ranger* sank, I was one of a number of CBC types taken by chopper to visit the rig for a day to get a first-hand look at the operation. The outing was organized by Mobil Oil. It was one hell of a scary workplace, the rig undulating in tandem with the North Atlantic swells, the surfaces slippery because of the wet wintry environment. I recall a terrifying incident in which one of the camera crew, a fellow named Murphy, suddenly lost his footing and dropped his hulking camera. You can imagine the cost to the corporation if it had actually fallen to the ground. Somehow, when he slipped, I instinctively shot out both my arms and the camera fell into them sending me to my knees. But it was saved. I was more than glad to get out of there at the end of the day.

On the night of the storm, I was home. It was like something out of the depths of hell, the house shaking and swaying so bad you didn't want to step off your front porch, let alone be out at sea.

I heard on the radio first thing in the morning what had happened and knew immediately that I would have to prepare fast for an evening news report. Other local reporters would file through the day for earlier newscasts, while my one responsibility was the big hit on *The National.* It was quite obvious the story was going to be a huge one.

Like a surgeon being faced suddenly with a knife-wound victim, there was no time for any sort of personal reaction on my part. You are just concerned with gathering up your tools and doing the job ahead of you. It was almost like springing to action as if by rote. By that time, I'd been a journalist for several years and discipline was part of the job. You just barrel ahead.

I felt a bit miffed after talking to Toronto, hearing that headquarters was flying in one of its heavyweights, Whit Fraser. I imagined they didn't have the confidence in me to cover such a huge news event alone. In the end, it was a smart move by CBC because there were too many angles for any one reporter to cover.

I've never been colder than on that day, the first day. It was a positively brutal, damp, bitter cold day. I'd wear my hat and then whip it off ever so briefly for the necessary on-air signoffs and the wind would cut into my ears. It was difficult to even speak because my lips were freezing up, too.

You have to realize, initially, very little real information was being given out. Mobil's PR people had whipped into action; Government and Coast Guard had their own communications personnel. Things were happening so fast it was difficult to organize a neat little news conference to bring media people up to speed, and we more or less followed the loci of action. Sometimes it was filming bodies being laid out on the dock at St. John's harbour, covered by tarps; sometimes it was out at the chopper pad at the airport where you would hope to find a SAR tech who might talk.

We did some interviews with family members. I remember that as they wept on camera, I began to feel the power of TV and the difference between it as a medium and print journalism. They didn't even need to speak, their tears said it all. The crassness of it hit me when our camera lens began to fog up after coming in to film from outside. I needed one man's tears to communicate to the rest of the country how the disaster had impacted this province, and technical difficulties were getting in the way. It was so awkward and shallow.

On a big story like that, as a reporter, you often save thoughts and feelings for later, focusing only on the task at hand and getting it done. I adopted this posture for days, just concentrating on getting the necessary video and gathering information.

The dam finally broke when I covered the first funeral. We were filming right in the church, and I was asked politely to leave out of respect for the family. Something just clicked, as though I had discovered a moral compass that temporarily had gone missing. We immediately moved to the roof of a nearby building, for exterior shots only.

Later, after putting together that report, I went home, exhausted, and it suddenly hit me. It was the first time I stopped to think about what had actually happened to those poor souls out there that night, and I felt that in trying to do my job I had forgotten to respect their families' privacy. I lost it and cried for hours and hours. Once I started, it took a long time to stop.

Part II: Gerry Phelan; Reporter, Q-Radio

ecause Q-Radio was a small newsroom with few employees, I ended up covering the story right from the beginning. When I got to the station on Monday morning, there was a hustle and bustle like never before, the wire clipping of short lines that there was a serious problem with one of the offshore oil rigs. The manager and I, along with another young reporter, agreed that, with the weather like it was, conditions on the North Atlantic were surely severe. That whole industry was a mystery to us, and my immature journalistic mind thought that whatever was going on, the all-powerful companies would keep it hush-hush. Thinking back, we almost seemed naïve.

I got on the phone and made the usual calls—Search and Rescue, Mobil Oil—and recorded a short interview: *Yes, there's a problem and weather's posing difficulties. Very little we can say now, but stay in touch. We're setting up a press conference.*

Things quickly worsened, moment by moment, and reports started coming in that a rig had sunk.

God, the prospect of that was horrifying to us.

Shorty before nine o'clock, I was out the door. It began a seemingly endless sequence of events.

Mobil Oil turned the Holiday Inn into a media centre. With so many reporters there it was a battle just to find a place to sit, and even worse trying awkwardly to get to the podium with my huge microphone flag. They had converged on St. John's from all over the world and here I was, a rookie, from this little middle-of-nowhere radio station. I felt so out of place.

Right from square one, there was a grave feeling. Mobil's officials offered very little in the way of solid facts: the *Ocean Ranger* had dropped off the radar, there was no word of survivors, but lights were seen in the water. Before long, Mobil's head honchos arrived. Then the dire words came: *The* Ocean Ranger *is lost and we can't hold out much hope for survivors.*

I felt sick.

Their area manager, Steve Romanski, had genuine tears in his eyes, the lines on his face drawn.

The media became like a pack of wolves. *What was being done? When were the names going to be released? What would settlements be worth?*

Those company officials faced a tough time, worse than they probably deserved.

Word then started to spread that a Russian ship was also in distress. Putting two and two together, the assumption was that perhaps it'd come too close to the rig and snapped an anchor chain. But those were just rumours.

That evening, a friend from the university called. He had a document inadvertently picked up at the news conference. He read part of it and agreed to drop it off. It was a Mobil briefing and obviously internal. *Survivors alive in the water. Crews bailing water from lifeboats. Supply vessel may have rammed a lifeboat.*

Scary stuff...

I called my manager. He insisted the story, as an exclusive, had to be broken, and we agreed to meet at the station the next morning to consult with our lawyer.

An official with Mobil had gotten wind of what we were up to and phoned my house with a veiled threat that if we were to run it there would be consequences. I wasn't thinking about court action, just the companies: the Seven Sisters overturning countries and mafia reprisals. Although it concerned me, I felt I had a job to do.

The next morning the story hit the airwaves.

We were affiliated with a national wire and voice service, broadcast news. They used it. Other media called requesting interviews. We had a printing company downstairs and quickly ran off dozens of copies for just about anyone who wanted them.

Because the majority of the men on the rig were Newfoundlanders, we felt there was a responsibility to inform our listeners of what was going on. It wasn't like today. There was no Internet, no satellite trucks, no email. We were their source of news—a direct connection. For the guy working at ESSO or driving across the Trans-Canada Highway, we were their link. But it was the wrong decision to release that document. The media makes mistakes all the time. Every day I hear we went with something that wasn't quite right, and you question what you did. Maybe I should've questioned myself more then, too.

It was still early when the names were released. I rushed to grab my copy, got to the nearest pay phone and went live. If there's been a car accident, names are very important—people want to know who is dead. I've always called it "clothesline news." You know, you're in your backyard and you talk over the clothesline with your neighbour about *so-and-so* and *Billy up the street.* As I read all eighty-four, I recognized a few, but everyone knew someone on the rigs. Years later, someone might say, "He was on the *Ranger*. We went to school with him." Even today, there's that emotional connection to the names. A young girl once took a tour of the station. Somehow I realized her father had died on the rig, and it brought back a whole host of memories. That's why, when I read those names, I was just about crying: they were real people and not just statistics on a piece of paper. I remembered reading somewhere that journalists weren't supposed to have feelings and tried to keep my head about me as best I could, but my emotions were raw and real.

That was the hardest day.

That evening, the provincial government held its own press conference on the eighth floor of the Confederation Building, the Cabinet Room. It was noisy with reporters setting up equipment and banging on typewriters, and then the place went dead silent when Premier Peckford sat down and started reading. Everyone expected him to appoint a Royal Commission to inquire into the loss of the rig. When he revealed the *Ranger* had listed just one week before, I thought I'd been punched in the stomach. The thing that sticks out more than the rest: "Conditions offshore are not severe enough to cause a shutdown." *My God*, I thought. *Are lives worth nothing?*

That week was my first taste of the national and international media and the pressures and responsibilities of the business. But our priority should've been to be right, not first. The grief I may have caused some families taught me the important lesson of how uncaring we can sometimes be.

I've learned well.

"No questions, please," Susan Sherk tells reporters during a press conference at the Holiday Inn. It was here that the *Rangers*'s crew list was first released.

RESPONSIBILITY AND REGRET
Susan Sherk; Senior Staff Coordinator, Mobil Oil Canada

Although I never thought of myself as a writer, when Mobil Oil called, I was doing a magazine, *Deck's Awash*, which was all about the province, and I had this idea that we'd feature every single community and its people. Petroleum development was a new industry here, still in the exploratory faze but moving towards development. Very few people had been hired. They wanted someone who understood Newfoundland and could help them translate the values of its people to their company.

My role with the company became educational—it was not technical. I oversaw internal communications and community-based consultations, which meant, and this is part of all environmental assessments today, spending a lot of time in schools and engaging the public and getting their input while helping them understand what the industry was and what it could possibly mean. People stuff.

I was at Mobil a year—it was not that long.

I lived on Forest Avenue, which was very close to downtown. That night I was with a friend who worked for CBC. We were making Valentine presents for our respective spouses. She went home around eleven o'clock before the storm really picked up. The next time I saw her we were at the Holiday Inn and she was interviewing me.

Shortly after one in the morning, I got a call from the office to say that there was an emergency. They couldn't tell me what, only that I had to come down, quick. So I threw on some clothes and jumped in the car.

At that point, we didn't know anything other than the *Ocean Ranger* was in some serious trouble. Things didn't look good.

I've done a lot of emergency procedures for companies. What happens is, you take a role. Mine was communications—I became a specialist overnight.

The most important thing was to get hold of the families to notify them that there was an issue offshore. The other was to ensure we had contact with all the various companies under contract to Mobil. Because we didn't own the rig—we only had a few people aboard—we didn't have a master crew list. The concern was the amount of time it would take to contact families before anything else occurred or they heard the news on the radio. Some guys lived in St. John's, but many elsewhere, while others had no fixed address. We arranged as best we could for the contractors to contact the families of all their employees and inform them of what was happing.

I was also responsible for setting up a telecommunications system in the office to deal with a large number of incoming calls while having a separate line to make outgoing calls. I went right to the top and contacted the president of Newfoundland Telephone. "We have an emergency. We don't know the extent of it but we need to get lines in right away." He was on it immediately. Soon we had a local staff employed to provide whatever updated information we had.

Valuable time was still lost that first day, one area where things could've been handled better.

We learned early that morning the rig was gone and that there was no hope of any survivors.

Regardless of possible legal ramifications, Mobil decided to meet the disaster head-on, whereas ODECO essentially closed its doors. They realized that everyone in Newfoundland was affected, and regardless of what was going to happen they had to respond in an appropriate way. When a company can understand that and translate it into action it makes a big difference, particularly to the families.

With the assistance of our public relations person, I ensured we had a place set up off-site for the families to receive regular updates on the status of what we knew was verifiable information. This was done regularly in the morning and at four in the afternoon. We couldn't have them in the bowels of the operation, while at the same time deal with the crisis at hand. Bill Mason, the president of Mobil Oil Canada, got on a plane from Calgary and came down. He met with everyone up front but didn't interfere with what was going on. Company managers are best used to meet with the media and act as the face of the company so that the public can see they're taking the situation very seriously. I've seen companies in disasters where the president never goes before the cameras, and the public become very skeptical and suspicious.

The national and international media had a feeding frenzy, and it became very difficult to try and keep them at bay. We were constantly asked to speculate, but we couldn't possibly do that. For a long time, the company was asked whether or not they withheld information. But in terms of facts, we made everything public. We just couldn't get sidetracked with other discussions because it was difficult enough ensuring the information we released was verifiable. A lot of my time was spent trying to protect the families from the media and preventing certain situations from occurring. Our saving grace was Scotty Morrison, who agreed to be a spokesperson for them. That relieved so much pressure on everyone.

The more experienced journalists understood what was at stake and that they could get their story without being too intrusive. When the supply boats were coming back, some hounded us to talk with the crews. One guy understood what they had gone through, that they'd just come off this horrific time doing salvage and recovery. "I really want to get my story, but I'll wait until they've gone home and been with their families. Then would it be possible?" When they operated with that kind of professionalism, we could accommodate them.

One of the most upsetting things was when I read the names of the eighty-four men on television. To this day I haven't seen the footage. The Holiday Inn was very crowded, and the cameras were stuck up in my face. At some point, I looked up and smiled. It was an inadvertent, nervous smile. I wasn't smiling for any reason—it was a nervous reaction, nothing more than that. The cameraman for CBC—I later learned his son, a diver, was one of the victims—was emotionally raw and rightfully went aboard me. I was devastated. If I could ever live my time over again, change that one thing I most regret, that would be it. But it just happened.

The days were all the same and yet different, melting into one long exhausting week. You forget about what you look like when you're before a news camera, and whether or not you've eaten that day. My mother, who was in the United States, saw me on national television. "You looked terrible!" she told me. "How can you be on television wearing blue jeans?"

It was the little things that meant a lot and helped everyone get through the worst of it. Everyone seems to have a story. For me, it was my daughter. A young teenager, she knew no one was leaving the office and that we had to order takeout just to get by. I loved crabmeat and she came down one day with some fresh clothes and my favourite crabmeat sandwich. I thought, *What a kid!*

Mobil knew they had to let their employees leave, if not we would start to think we were too important to the whole operation and without us everything would fall apart. When I finally did go home on Friday afternoon, I crawled out of Atlantic Place, got in my car and turned left, which was the wrong way. I was so disoriented I couldn't remember where my house was. A policeman stopped me. I told him I had just spent five days dealing with the *Ocean Ranger* disaster. I hadn't cried the whole time, but when he asked me if he could drive me home, I lost it. I had to lose it—I realized that later. I worked so hard that when I stopped I just fell to pieces.

There was a period in my life when I felt somehow responsible for what had happened. People on the outside assumed the company was totally corrupt and driven solely by greed, an "us and them" mentality. But it was truly a community disaster, and many of us were directly impacted. My neighbour's husband was the first body brought ashore. Although we would later become dear friends, I became a kind of lightning rod for what she had gone through, and she let loose her frustrations on me because she was so young and pregnant. It was all very tough. Over time, that barrier seemed to disappear.

A MONOLOGUE ABOUT IT NEVER BEING EASY
*Ray Hawco; Director of Community and Public Relations,
Newfoundland and Labrador Petroleum Directorate*

spent twenty years in rural Newfoundland as a Roman Catholic priest—my parish stretching along the entire length of the Bonavista Peninsula—and knew a lot of guys on the rigs. Many of them started calling me because I worked for the Petroleum Directorate. According to them, there were problems. I mentioned this to Steve Milan, my boss. He wanted to know what their issues were and told me to listen and give them a forum. I met with the boys on a number of occasions, at a bar and a restaurant and someone's home. Sometimes there would be ten or twelve and other times more. There was no protection for them and they were thinking about starting up a union, but for the lack of something better hoped I'd take their message back to government and then on to the companies. They talked about the difficulties working offshore, but the worst message seemed to come from the *Ocean Ranger*: intimidation, a general lack of training on the drill floor, and inadequate safety drills. I told my superiors things weren't as they seemed.

Instructed to go out and familiarize myself with the three rigs, I subsequently spent several months on *Sedco 706* and *Zapata Ugland*. On February 14, there were sixteen of us suiting up at the hanger waiting to head out to the *Ocean Ranger* when a guy came over to me. It was Gerald Clark from Easteel. "Three of us got a contract to head out this weekend, and now I'm told only two of us can go. If all of us can't go, none of us are." I let him take my place. I was supposed to leave on the next chopper, but with weather having taken a real sour turn, I decided to put it off.

At about 3:30 the next morning, I received a call from the office and was told the *Ocean Ranger* was in some serious trouble.

When I got in, there was already a meeting in progress. Representatives from Mobil Oil, RCMP, RNC, Department of Justice and the Department of Health were there assessing the situation based on the information available. The picture looked pretty bleak and it was thought the rig was gone. Although a contingency plan was in place, we were never so pessimistic as to plan for total disaster.

Written guidelines about what to do next didn't exist. The focus quickly shifted to the families.

That became my responsibility.

I was to set up some system of notification. As a former Roman Catholic priest, I had dealt with countless tragedies. For five years, I was on the road all the time, travelling eight thousand miles a month, and was at the scene of a lot of major fatalities around Bonavista Bay. There are places on the highway I still pass and remember what happened: Port Blanford, four people killed; North Brook, three people; Grand Falls, a young woman; Thorburn Lake Overpass, a truck driver. But especially the Clarenville area—there was a lot of them.

I recommended we notify the families through the churches. The message to be conveyed was a dreadful one: *The rig is gone, and you should prepare for the worst.*

I immediately contacted the heads of all the churches, most of whom I knew personally. They each allocated someone to attend a meeting at the Petroleum Directorate where a course of action would be decided upon.

A full crew manifest wasn't available; all we had were names, no permanent addresses or contact information. Because of the settlement patterns of Newfoundland families and the relative isolation of outport communities, they determined as best they could the most likely religion of each person and where they were probably from. It wasn't too difficult. Heffernan, Foley, Noseworthy, O'Brien—those were surely Catholics from in and around town somewhere. But what about a name like Freid? That didn't sound Catholic or Anglican or United. So there were difficulties. Twenty-eight of the crew were from outside the province and we weren't even sure how to make contact with their families. Thankfully, the Salvation Army stepped in and agreed they would take care of those situations.

By Tuesday morning, most of the families had been contacted. For them, it came as a real shock.

Some just didn't want to accept it. I started to receive calls late in the night from families fearing survivors could be trapped somewhere in the sunken rig. Jack Jacobsen's family called three times one night: "There has to be a move made to get down into that diving chamber. There's got to be something done before they freeze to death or suffocate." Other families from the US called, too. But how could I explain to someone in Louisiana what the North Atlantic is like in February when they can see a rig from their front deck? There was nothing anyone could do. People were frustrated and would hang up and curse on you because you weren't giving them the answers they wanted. Some were convinced you weren't doing anything. To them, I must've sounded just like another hard and cold creature of the government.

With eighty-four crewmen, it was assumed there would be a lot of bodies—certainly forty or fifty. It didn't happen that way. We started to get them in two or three at a time. Thirteen was the most.

Right away, problems arose with identification. After preliminary work by the RCMP, all the employers were taken by the RNC to view photographs and then to the morgue itself. Each body was covered with a sheet and brought into the viewing room on a wheeled table. No one could make a definite identification and some insisted on returning several times.

ODECO had so many people on board, over sixty guys, that it was impossible for their managers to know all the names and faces. I got a call from Gordon Noseworthy, one of the *Ranger*'s off-duty crewmen. His brother, Randy, had gone down on the rig. I'm not sure how he got the message, maybe through the public media—I didn't take many notes, and Gordon is dead now—but we knew each other pretty well through our meetings. "Look, I know all of them," he explained. "I can identify anyone." Gordon recognized the man and from then on made himself available to view the bodies before any of the employers. He could usually provide identification or at least narrow it down to a few possibilities.

Down at the dock, we talked quite a bit. He was very concerned about his brother's young family. Every time he went down and opened up a body bag he was hoping and praying it'd be his brother, for the sake of Roslyn and the kids. That was scary for him. But he never once hesitated, and when I'd call him, maybe three or four times in the course of a night, he'd be just as cooperative as ever. That's the kind of guy he was, an average Joe with a good heart and a kind soul. What was so difficult for him made it a little easier for everyone else.

There were off-the-shelf kinds of things I did when the body was damaged and we weren't too sure who it was. We simply couldn't have the next-of-kin come down. Once, we had a tentative identification. I knew a guy here in the Goulds who shared the same surname. His father had worked for a Charlie Bells or a Charlie Gough I once bought an outboard motor from. At least, that's how I remember it. Through that contact, I asked if they were related and who might be the best person to make the positive ID. It had to be someone strong and who could take it better; I didn't want to have to involve the parents. The circumstances were always a little different, but I went about it the same way. The first time, I met a brother downtown for a beer. I had a ring and took it out and just twirled it between my fingers. I didn't have to say anything—he just knew. Other times it was a chain, a medal, and once it was a belt buckle.

A definitive identification was always made at the Health Sciences Complex, sometimes by a close friend, while for others it was a family member. Eric Pike was the chief forensic pathologist. He was very precise and professional, a real cool individual, but once he dealt with the families he was completely compassionate and made it at least bearable for them. He was unbelievable. We asked the contractors to be there to offer condolences and to pay for the funeral expenses. We couldn't have the families tormented with those sorts of trivial things when they were already going through so much.

It was hard on the company men, too. Right up until Monday night, Max Ruelokke held out hope for survivors and kept relaying that message to the families. Having lost five of his divers, five good friends, he felt he had a real responsibility to them. There was an incident Wayne Miller was involved in, and Max had sent him out again to make up for it. He agonized over that, over everything—he went through a horrible ordeal.

Right at the end, two bodies were found. They were from Eaststeel—welders. One was the guy who took my place on the chopper only a week before. But no one knew who they were and a number of the contractors came down to the morgue. ODECO was under considerable pressure. It was their rig and most of the men had been their employees. They were constantly going back and forth between Pier 17 and the Health Sciences Complex, the media trailing right behind them. This time, Blondie Gernandt, the onshore supervisor, snapped and took a swing at me in the waiting room. Realizing the bodies of his close friends wouldn't be found, as far as he was concerned, that was the last straw.

I've dealt with a lot of tragedies in my life. You never become inured to them, but you somehow enable yourself to be strong, calm and compassionate. You get the strength to do it—not to sleep, not to eat. You have to, for the families. I've seen others do it, too. People can go days and days without really considering themselves. When I finally came home, I slept all that night and didn't wake up until eleven o'clock the next evening. My doctor explained to me that I was on an extreme high, my adrenaline was pumping, and once the barrel was empty, it was empty. Although you have to have the desire to do it and want to help, it's still never easy.

A MONOLOGUE ABOUT BARELY CATCHING YOUR BREATH
Gary Browne; Director of Emergency Measures (Acting),
Royal Newfoundland Constabulary

We were lucky, if I can use a word like that for such a sad and horrible time. St. John's was an insular community—everyone knew everyone—and if I've learned anything from all my years as a police officer it's that the bottom line always comes down to people. A big mainland city like Toronto or Montreal might have money, but when you know most everyone involved, the go-to people, you get things done. That's why we were more sensitive to the human cost of the tragedy. It was a hard time for everyone.

I was a young officer with the Royal Newfoundland Constabulary, had ten years service under my belt, and on leave from the Criminal Investigation Division to Emergency Measures. Although there were contingency plans in place for storms, electrical outages and flooding, as well as a whole host of other possible problems, I was sent to complete their *Major Emergency Manual*, which would cover every aspect of field operations.

That February, the director was out of the province, leaving me on call.

I was living on Marine Drive in Torbay with my wife and kids. At around four in the morning, the phone rang. As a police officer, you get used to being woken at all hours—it usually meant trouble.

My wife answered. After a brief pause, she said, "Just one moment, please."

It was an official from Mobil Oil. "Mr. Browne, are you the Acting Director of Emergency Measures?"

"Yes, I am."

"I have some bad news. The *Ocean Ranger* is in trouble, and it doesn't look good."

I took a long breath. "Okay, I'll look after it."

Splashing some water across my face, I got out a notepad and started making calls. The first was to the Department of Justice. I was asked to pick up the minster and his deputy at the Confederation Building and make our way to Atlantic Place through the snow and blazing wind.

From the moment we got there, you could tell it was the worst kind of a disaster. People were running around, the phones were ringing off the hook. Things were going crazy.

I bumped into Ray Hawco, an official with the Petroleum Directorate and a man I had a deep respect for—he's such a kind, caring individual. Word had come in that the rig had gone down—I can't remember exactly what was said, but it was negative, heavy stuff—and there was a serious concern about how to notify families. For them, uncertain of what was happening, minutes would surely seem like days. Ray, a former Catholic priest, contacted clergy from the various denominations and asked them to come down. Seeing them in action in that boardroom was something else, I tell you. For the Newfoundland victims—they were from all over, from every nook and cranny of the province—details were sketchy, but as soon as a surname was mentioned, and with no phonebook or directory there to assist them, they knew the man's church, where he was from and what family he belonged to. I don't think they were wrong once.

If it took a long while to get the names out, it's because they had to be double checked and triple checked. I can only imagine how it was interpreted on the other side.

The tragedy then took on another horrible dynamic when a Russian cargo ship sank in the same area as the *Ranger*. It created complicated ripple effects. Families were calling with the hope of finding out what was going on, and with everyone doing their best, trying to get it right, a Russian fishing vessel appeared on the scene and started picking up bodies. The fear was that they could be guys from the rig, our guys.

Can you imagine the uproar if a Canadian, a Newfoundlander, was taken back to Russia?

The Minister of Justice, negotiating through External Affairs, requested they come to St. John's to be properly identified. I was sent to represent the provincial government, and RCMP Staff Sergeant Bob Penny, the Feds. Bob and I, God rest his soul, were neighbours and played on the same softball team together down in the East End. He was a dedicated police officer and a wonderful friend.

When we boarded the Russian vessel, accompanied by a local translator, it was quite tense. Walking up over the gangway, I noticed from the corner of my eye bodies laid out on the deck and covered with tarp. I was in the forces for some time, and the first thing that came to mind was the militaristic fashion of those fishermen. I didn't know much about Russians but figured they'd done some compulsory service because they were all stood off in a hollow square, a drill, as if at attention.

We went to the wheelhouse. The captain was there with his two mates and another stern looking chap. We'd ask questions through the interpreter and he'd always look across to this other guy for the proper answer. It was obvious *he* was the one calling the shots and not the captain.

"We need to get the bodies ashore," I explained. "They have to be properly identified."

It then got touchy.

The Russians felt they were theirs, not Canadians from the rig. Hours of negotiations went on.

Eventually, they relented: "Our men will not be touched by anyone—we'll take them."

In my mind's eye, I can still see the bodies laid out in the temporary morgue and covered and the tags attached, the identification team going from gurney to gurney checking for personal effects, taking fingerprints and pictures. The survivor we had looking at them wouldn't identify one. I couldn't understand it—still don't—because it wasn't a huge boat, maybe thirty or forty men at sea together for weeks and months on end. We were there for hours asking who the person was, if he'd been on the ship. A day passed before he made the positive ID.

It was the responsibility of the Constabulary to maintain a perimeter, and officers would come to me saying that the media were at the gate demanding to be let in to take pictures. People were dead and their loved ones were waiting to hear news—there was no way I was going to let that happen, zooming in on bodies whatever condition they were in. I couldn't tell you how many times someone was going to have my job. Old stuff like *these are Gestapo tactics* were pretty common. Unfortunately, there was no way of preventing their cameras from snapping shots from the Battery. But it could've been worse.

Newfoundlanders weren't used to that, which was why when someone suggested we get meat trucks to store remains in, just about everyone, right up to the top levels of government, weren't going to have it.

You could see that wasn't going to be tolerated. Bodies coming in on the supply boats would be put in individual hearses. I was very proud of that, the tremendous respect given to the dead. It might sound naïve, but for us, Newfoundlanders, it starts when you're a kid and you go to a cemetery and your parents say, "Don't walk across that grave. Someone is buried there." It was something like that.

When a supply ship was just outside the Narrows, we'd go down and stand and wait at the dock. It was so damn cold and the wind so high, the harbour half frozen in ice. I can still feel the shivers going up through the soles of my boots. With a hearse parked beside us, we'd be dressed in parkas and our hoods pulled tight, but the little bit of exposed skin would sting and burn and you could barely catch your breath.

The first time, the sheet had just slipped down a bit. I saw his face, and it struck me like a ton of bricks. He had been my boyhood friend. He and I had gone to St. Bon's together right to Grade 8, grew up in the same area of Georgetown—he on Maxi Street and I on Belvedere Street—just a few hundred yards apart. We played basketball and handball in the courts outside school and often walked home together.

"Oh, my God...." It was all I could say.

After a moment, I said who it was. The other constable, who also knew him, wasn't so sure.

"It's him, it's him," I said. "Without a doubt it's him."

We called his sister to have someone come down. Sure enough, I was right.

I then found out his wife was pregnant.

Even today, if I'm tired or stressed out about something, I often wake from nightmares. It's the recurring dream of seeing that whole episode, his face, played out again in my mind like a movie. I never met his wife or his child, but it's stuck with me a lifetime. This is the first time I've spoken of it since then.

A few days later, it was three or four in the morning, maybe close to dawn, I can't remember, and several of us, all young family men, were standing in the dark, waiting. A hand slipped from beneath the sheet. There was a ring, a wedding band. Although I can still see it so plainly, I find it hard to explain, even now. It sparkled, shone like a beacon of light. No one said anything, just looked at one another. Years later, I spoke to a few of those guys and they all said they felt the same thing: *There but for the grace of God go I.*

As a police officer, you try and keep your emotions out of it and not let them interfere with your work, but you're not a robot, you can't shut it off like a light switch—you're human. You're running on adrenaline—something stimulates you and you react—but every now and again I would stop and go off by myself and try to get it together. We're all different, but emergency responders are very caring people, and I could see that same stress on everyone's face. There's a whole host of emotions running through you.

No one wanted to give up. I was young and worried about whether or not I could step up to the plate and do what was necessary for the victim's families and the force. In my heart, I felt like I did all that I possibly could, still do, and it's natural to doubt yourself. Talking about it now is part of the healing process.

THOSE FAMILIES THAT I KNEW PERSONALLY
Rev. Bert Cheeseman; Rector, Parish of Petty Harbour;
The Anglican Diocese of Eastern Newfoundland and Labrador

For a time, I presided over the Anglican parish of Eastport. One evening, two carpenters who worked in St. John's failed to turn up. There was a general sense of alarm, and I went to see their families. It was no time after that when the RCMP phoned. The driver had fallen asleep at the wheel and crossed over into the oncoming lane. They'd been hit head-on by a transport truck, their car totally demolished. That came as a real shock; the family were just looking for them, had their supper cooked and on the table and everything.

I was prepared for whatever I was about to walk into that morning at Mobil Oil, but could never have imagined the sheer magnitude of the disaster.

What I found was confusion. Absolute confusion. No one knew what to do; certainly the staff didn't know what to do. It was frustrating. Ray Hawco had me and a few others down there, and we asked for the crew list, but there wasn't one available. I just couldn't believe that a company like that would be in such disarray that they wouldn't have the names and addresses of the guys on board the rig or their next of kin. It was days before we got full access to that information, and it was just through sheer hard work that we figured out exactly who was who. Sometimes we went through the payroll department, other times the contractors came forward, but mostly someone would say *this one went to Brother Rice,* or *that one's got a cousin in my parish.* All that took up a good bit of the morning.

Ray sat everyone down and we tried as best we could to set out a format of how we would notify the families and what we would say to them. I took ten or twelve names—something like that. "This is Reverend Bert Cheeseman. I'm calling on behalf of the Province of Newfoundland and Labrador and Mobil Oil. There's been a tremendous disaster: the *Ocean Ranger* went down last night. I believe you had a member of your family on board." The first thing they always wanted to know was if there were any survivors. "At this point in time we can't say with any certainty. We'll keep you informed as the day progresses."

A lot of the details are gone now—it's been twenty-seven years—but you remember the big things, important things: the families. The emotions are certainly still there and they'll never leave.

It was difficult trying to mask the fear you really felt inside. The first call I made was to a mother in Australia. I don't remember the name, but that's not important. When I told her, she broke down and went to pieces, and someone else came on the line. This was someone who meant a lot to them.

There were two with whom I was personally linked.

With the first, I knew the wife. She was a secretary at the school when I worked in Eastport. I didn't know her husband, Dominic, very well, because they'd just married. They had one child. The last time I spoke with her she was on cloud nine. She was in her early thirties, without much prospect of getting married and starting a family, when she met him. She was delighted. They had their whole lives in front of them.

On the phone, before I could say anything, she said, "I know. I know."

Just like that: *I know.*

"I have to tell you, Ruth, on behalf of the Province of Newfoundland and Labrador and Mobil Oil, and certainly myself, we extend.... What can I say to you, Ruth? Your dream is broken."

And that's what it was for her.

Only then, hours and hours later, did I realize Ken Chafe was out there, too. His parents were active members of my parish. The thing was, Ken and the other Eaststeel guys weren't even supposed to be out there. They'd gone out to do a welding job but got stuck in the storm. I called his mother and all she could say through her tears was that she didn't know what his family were going to do, his wife and children.

"When I get through here this evening, whatever time it is, I'll come see you."

When I walked into that house, I saw total devastation. It's the only word I can come up with to describe it.

One call came as a real shock. It was to a man in England, a father. "You have a son?" I asked.

"Yes," he said. "But I don't know where he is."

"No?"

"I haven't seen him in four or five years, and I don't give a good god-damn if I ever do again."

"Sir, there's the possibility that might be the case. He was working on the *Ocean Ranger*." He knew little of the rig, about the destruction that'd happened the night before.

"That's all right," he said. "He didn't care about us, and I'm as bloody well sure we don't care about him, either."

I managed to collect myself and ask him what he wanted to do if a body was recovered.

"I don't care. You can bury him wherever you like."

"Is his mother there?" It was my last shot at finding someone who cared for him.

"No," he barked. "She's gone; she's left." I got the impression they were divorced.

That call broke my heart. I couldn't believe that even though this father didn't know where his son was, and regardless of whether or not he'd sent them money, came home or called, he could be so cruel as to say he didn't care that he was dead.

Facing all of that, there was no way I could keep up with the day-to-day duties of my parish. I was in the thick of it and just couldn't get away from the Mobil office. It was like being an octopus with my tentacles spread out with each one doing something different, and if I let go I'd never be able to pick up the pieces again.

But I managed the Sunday services. Having gone through what I had gone through that week—was still going through—it put a cloud over me, and I couldn't help but talk about the shortness and uncertainty of human life. Even when I went to do a simple homily, something would trigger my emotions, and I'd feel compelled to talk about the tragedy. We all shared in that sadness, the whole congregation.

Ken Chafe's parents weren't there for that service. I know because I went to their home that evening. The whole family was there, just sat around waiting for news. It wasn't until days and days later that they finally got him—he was the last. After all that time, a week and a half, it was an immense relief which brought them some sense of closure. The hurt was there, but they now had a body and could have a funeral. With all the other fathers and sons out there that weren't picked up and didn't get found, they thought themselves pretty fortunate.

As things started to settle, and with no reassurances coming from Mobil or ODECO, the big concern, particularly for those women who had lost their husbands, the breadwinner, was survival. Ken's wife, with no job and three or four young children at home, faced a rough time. *How am I going to look after the kids? How am I going to pay the bills? How are we going to eat?*

The congregation realized she needed help, and everyone came together—the parish didn't have to organize a thing. For weeks, people took turns preparing food, and one person even donated five thousand dollars. I know because I issued the income tax receipt. He said, "I could do it, and I was glad to do it." But there were others who gave money, too.

In the end, Dominic's family weren't so lucky—there was no body.

"You're sure they're not going to get anyone else?" Ruth asked me. "You're sure they've looked everywhere?"

A memorial service was held but it brought no closure. When the family walked out they were as grieved as ever.

I spoke to Ruth then, before she left.

"I now know I have a lot of friends who care. None of these people will go home and forget me and my child. But even if I'm provided with all the money in the world, it won't fill this void within me. I'm the one who has to go on without him, the one to see our child grow up without a father. No one can carry this burden but me."

It's something I'll never forget.

Her husband had been the control room operator the night the rig sank, and the rumour surfaced that he was to blame for the sinking. It was on a good many people's minds. Ruth heard it and was terribly perturbed. When the inquiry started, she said to me, "Do you think you could go up and see what it's all about?" But whatever I learned I couldn't share because it would've only made her suffering that much worse.

I'll still see her from time to time. I think it's been so long now that she's accepted the fact that she's had to go on without him, that it wasn't the life she had anticipated, the life she had expected: "I've done the best I could."

With those families I knew, I was able to keep in contact with them for a period of about six months. I followed up pretty regularly, once or twice a week, dropping by to say hello and to ask how they were doing. You could see they weren't rebuilding their lives, that they were in a state of suspended animation. Like, here they were and this person was there, and now that he was gone they just couldn't continue on without him. It was painful to see. But if I helped one or two of those families cope, it was all worth it.

John O'Brien during a CBC open house, sometime in the mid-1980s.

A MONOLOGUE ABOUT A WITNESS
Marie Wadden; Reporter, CBC News: Here & Now

In 1979, when oil was first discovered on the Hibernia site, I was looking for a specialty at the CBC, something new, something with which I could distinguish myself apart from other reporters. I avidly sought out that beat and made it my own. I was there at the first news conference when Brian Peckford made the announcement, and then again when Leo Barry went before the cameras and held up that small vial of Hibernia crude. This new industry was supposed to mean a whole new way of life for Newfoundlanders, good fortune at last for the province with the worst unemployment rate in the country. For a long while, we basked in the promise of oil, and I covered just about every related story for the better part of five years.

Initially, my crew and I were sent to look at the social impact of offshore oil development on Northern Scotland, an area with a strong fishing industry not unlike our own, and then a press tour of *Sedco 709.* I did a lot of stories which raised red flags about the potential economic impact on traditional industries and the environment. But issues of safety were not something we focused on because of our limited access to the rigs and the fact that we were all just a bit agog at the technology.

My cameraman, John, had two sons working offshore on exploratory rigs. We were at odds because of my critical approach, which is the nature of this business when you have to approach all topics skeptically. He thought that this new industry was fantastic and was delighted at the opportunity it gave his sons which they might not have had otherwise.

On the night of February 14, I was invited to a friend's house at the Battery for supper. The kitchen was up on the second floor facing the harbour. While we ate, we were amazed, stunned at how high the waves were—the spray actually hit the window. We stayed overnight, and I woke earlier than usual. The morning news said that a rig on the Grand Banks was listing, and I rushed into work.

Climbing the stone steps on the east side of the building, I passed a man, a figure, standing out in the cold with a parka on and the hood pulled up over his face. Consumed with getting into the newsroom for an update, it didn't register. When I went in and talked to the night manager, he told me the *Ocean Ranger* was indeed listing badly and had been evacuated.

I thought again of the figure standing in the storm. I went out. "John, is that you?"

He turned towards me and I could see what he had been hiding behind that fur hood, his face filled with an incredible sorrow and fear.

I asked him if any of his sons were out there, aboard that rig. "Yes," he said, "my youngest."

Then, at that moment, it became so much more real to me.

Mobil Oil scheduled a news conference for that morning at the Holiday Inn. John insisted on covering it with my sound technician and I, and we supported that because we wanted him to be there to find out for himself exactly what was going on. Not long after we arrived, a friend who worked for the oil companies came up to me. "Marie, I don't think John should be here. It's not good news. Someone should take him home." I told this to our sound technician, who was closer to John than I, and the news conference was delayed while we got another cameraman.

When the announcement came, it was worse than anyone could've ever imagined.

In the coming days and months, it was through John's grief that I reported the story as it unfolded.

The CBC sent me to Boston for the first round of US Coast Guard public hearings, and then to New Orleans for the second. Immediately, you could smell the whiff of lawsuits in the air, the culture of litigation in full force, the company lawyers having descended. The emphasis was on the various parties involved escaping any culpability. Even after nine days of testimony, they were no further ahead in understanding the chain of events which led to the disaster.

The first eye witness testimony was heard there. It was the crew from one of the supply ships, the *Seaforth Highlander*. They had come upon a lifeboat. The crew threw lines, but it capsized, spilling the men into the water. Because of high waves and frigid temperatures, no one could be saved. That boat drifted away and was never recovered.

It was difficult in those days to get news back to Newfoundland quickly, especially film, and I had an artist in St. John's render drawings while I did a telephone recorded voice-over. It was primitive but very powerful, because the story itself was just so powerful. My colleagues told me later that when it aired on *Here & Now* they were attending a traditional seal supper to celebrate the start of the hunt. John had accompanied them. I can only imagine what he went through when they turned on the television, envisioning his son amongst the men in the water.

John was with me when I covered the Royal Commission, insisted on being there. Facing the inquiry panel just above the families and the lawyers, we would set up each morning on the balcony in St. Mary's Church on Craigmiller Avenue. Chief Justice Hickman allowed us to film the hearings in their entirety. Although there was the distance between the judiciary and the reporter, there was warmth and support from him in that he knew what we were doing was very important.

It quickly became apparent that the whole operation had been on very shaky grounds. The American company had come up here and put men like John's son at risk without survival suits, proper evacuation systems or training. I remember thinking, although I never spoke it, that for him it must've been a great betrayal, having placed such trust and faith in the industry that was going to mean so much for his sons in starting their lives.

John, a stoic kind of guy, never spoke much about his feelings. But he was so courageous to stand there with his camera in position, tears streaming down his face, listening day after day to the examples of carelessness on the part of the company and all the pieces they had not put in place. He was a sentinel in the way that he stood at that tripod witnessing the event through his job, every aspect of what had happened. But while it was so personal for him, he never once made a decision through his photography that editorialized. There was no interference on his part with the truth telling, because that's what he was, a witness.

Although I was thirty-two, young, with no children, able to devote a lot of my personal life to the story, it was still very difficult.

Everything I saw and everything I had heard impacted me. But I forced myself not feel. What right did I have to feel anything? I couldn't allow myself to feel sorry when I hadn't lost anyone, when every day people like John were suffering through it all. I just couldn't compare anything I felt to what they were going through.

Always top news, the line editor would leave a spot trusting I'd have a story. There were often pictures of the families and the awful image of the overturned lifeboat, the debris at the site, video of the broken porthole. Right up until the last day, I remember driving back to the CBC building knowing I had to get the story out because we were going on air in an hour, but wondering how I could possibly do that.

John and I didn't work together very often after the inquiry because we changed cameramen every day. Unless there was a continuing story, our paths would've crossed only occasionally.

But offshore oil was still my beat. I was sent to Norway to do a series on safer evacuation systems on rigs in the North Sea, and how much power workers' unions had in affecting public policy. My cameraman—the sound technician who'd accompanied me to that first Mobil press conference—had to get pictures from a helicopter of the five platforms that were in operation, and I remember how shocked he was when they opened up a hatch in the bottom and attached him to a safety harness so he could shoot down. He was terrified, but did it. I sometimes think he acted with a sense of mission because of what had happened to John's son.

When I left Newfoundland to take another job in television, John and I lost track. He died shortly thereafter. But I know his life was never the same. I saw him lose a lot of joy after the *Ocean Ranger* went down—the whole thing took the good out of him.

John deserved to see Ken succeed.

PART 4
THE LONGEST WEEK

If I lose my husband, am I still a wife? If I lose my children, am I still a mother? Who am I? To walk into that house and to know that bed will never be occupied by that person again; to go to their closets and feel their clothes and smell them; to go through your cookbooks and see you're going through these recipes that were their favourites; to listen to a song that you knew was one of their favourites. What do you do with all that? It's so full and so empty at the same time.
— Lata Pada, wife and mother of Air India disaster victims; from the film *Air India 182*

God bless and strengthen all the grieved in Newfoundland.
— Nish Collin, "Requiem and Respect," *The Daily News*, February 17, 1982

Surely God is my salvation; I will trust, and will not be afraid, for the Lord God is my strength and my might; he has become my salvation.
— *Isaiah 12:2*, first reading at the ecumenical memorial service, February 19, 1982

The body of Mel Freid was the first to be recovered. National and international media filmed mourners as they left his funeral at St. Pius X. The footage was later played on the evening news.

A MONOLOGUE ABOUT BEING THE FIRST
Annmari, a wife

Mel and I were close like a long-married couple and planned a life together with our unborn child. But because he died at just thirty-two, there was no sense of a life being closed gently. He was so loved, and not just by me, but by a large circle of friends. Even after all this time, twenty-seven years, they still talk about him. It brings a smile to my face.

We met at a party in Toronto. At the time, he was going to university in Ottawa, and I had just moved there from St. John's.

The next day, a few of us needed a lift to go horseback riding. Somebody said, pointing to Mel, "That guy's got a car."

So I went up to him. "Ah... wanna go horseback riding? Oh, and by the way, we need your car."

That's how we met.

We soon started hanging out and then began dating. For us, things came together pretty easy. We were both from St. John's and went to school together. We shared mutual friends and my parents knew his. In those days, everybody from St. John's knew one another.

I was very lucky. Mel had a wonderful sense of humour and always had everyone in stitches. As soon as he walked into a party it started, like it was on hold just for him. And you'd never hear anyone say anything negative about him, either—he was just too nice a guy.

When we came home, we got married and bought an old house on Leslie Street which we decided to rescue. A lot of time was spent finishing floors, putting up walls and building a deck, with one inspiring the other through the drudgeries and difficulties.

When the opportunity to work offshore came up, Mel was helping his father run their surplus store. I wasn't crazy about his parents. His father had led him along for too long on the promise that he'd let him take over the business, and years went by without it materializing. We knew people who were working in the oil patch—my brother-in-law owned an offshore supply company—and Mel was offered the job of Supplies Manager with ODECO. That was the summer of 1981.

I was glad he took it. You couldn't get a job for love nor money when I came out of university. It's not like today where employers are begging for workers.

I used to drop him off at the heliport to catch the flight out and pick him up three weeks later. He wasn't wild about working on the *Ocean Ranger*. He missed his friends, his life here, and found it rather restrictive. I think his wonderful sense of humour carried him through a lot.

The week the rig sank, Mel started his shift a few days early. It was supposed to be his last, and he was then going to work for the company at their St. John's office.

The weather was horrible on Valentine's Day. Living in an old house, I could hear the wind batter the windows and the siding. I had this awful feeling in me, too, like I didn't belong in my own skin. I wasn't surprised when he didn't call—although he always called—figuring they had enough to deal with already. I woke at six in the morning, which was very strange for me. Before I went out to shovel the driveway, I heard a short blurb on the radio about trouble on the Grand Banks. But it didn't really register.

At work, students were talking about things they'd heard—nothing definitive, nothing concrete, just rumours. I didn't want to listen to any of it and went off with some colleagues for coffee. That's when my brother came in. He took me aside and said, "I want you to come home."

I figured I'd be better off working, to keep my mind off things, but he eventually convinced me.

As the day slipped into the afternoon and then into evening, we still hadn't heard exactly what had happened but knew it was bad. I thought, *If anyone is going to survive it'll be Mel. He knows the outdoors, he's used to survival. He sells all that sort of stuff.*

Then we got the call.

Mel's body was the first to be found. He was identified by a friend down at the dock. As it turned out, he must've given his survival suit to someone else, because he was found without his. Not that it would've helped out there in the freezing cold.

I went into a daze. I remember sitting in the living room crying and my mother coming in. I remember looking after my brother's kids. I don't remember a lot after that.

I had a wake for Mel, a funeral, and people came to the house. Friends brought dishes and dishes of food. Specifics, I couldn't say. I remember the skirt and blouse I wore, a few other things, and that's about it. When I was a child, if a hearse passed, people would stop and make the sign of the cross. Everyone stopped on the Parkway as we drove from the funeral home to the church, everyone. I can picture that like it was yesterday. The funeral was at St. Pius X, where we were married. It was overflowing—people were standing everywhere. It amazed me.

I spent the better part of ten years with Mel, up to that point my entire adult life, and then he was gone. He was a big part of a lot of people's lives, and not just mine, but this huge circle of friends we had. And he wasn't much different than the rest of the guys who died. Most of them were his age, some older, some younger. It was a big part of humanity gone, just like that.

I was twenty-eight and six weeks pregnant when the *Ranger* sank, about to raise an orphan. I knew from my friends and family the difficulties of bringing up a child with two parents, and was scared to death to have to do it alone. I wouldn't have Mel there during the pregnancy, the labour, the delivery, or through the baby's life. I would lose so much: his reaction to the birth and the baby's development.

Lexi was born six months later.

Not long after, I went back to work at the university and sold the house. Without Mel, I just didn't have it in me to continue fixing it up. More than that, I'd have to look at the things he did or wanted to do which would disturb and upset me. That's when I moved to Montreal to do a degree at McGill. At the same time, I had to go through a court case with the companies. Fighting for money, for restitution from worker's compensation, was horrible. It took us two long years.

I don't know how I coped, I truly don't. Although I faced a lot of lonely nights, I had to carry on.

Mel's been dead for so long now. It's a generation ago, a whole other life. Had he lived, I wouldn't have done those other degrees, wouldn't have lived abroad and travelled. But I'd give it all up to go back to what I had. But you can't... you can't...

God, I miss him.

Ron Heffernan in Edmonton, Alberta. "As soon as the snow starts falling, I think of him," said his sister, Elaine.

A UNIQUE BOND
Elaine, a sister

I was working for the Crown corporation NORDCO when somebody at the office said Mobil Oil was hiring. I was quite happy
where I was but figured I should check it out and sent in a resume.
Not expecting to get an interview—I'd done it on the spur of the
moment, hadn't put much thought into it—a few days later, I got a
call and went down and was introduced to the drilling manager, Merv
Graham. If hired, this was who I'd be working for, the HR person
explained.

He seemed like a very nice, sociable man, but because the operation
was just getting underway, we were constantly being interrupted. At
some point, I said, "If I was your secretary, you wouldn't be bothered
like this—I'd handle everything outside your door."

I was offered the job. That was in April 1980.

Immediately, what struck me was the money. More money than I
could've ever imagined was being spent on oil exploration. There was
a lot of excitement, too, excitement about what it meant for the company, for the province. And you felt like you were part of what was
going on, not just a secretary.

The year before, two of my brothers, Ron and Ray, went to Calgary
to look for work. They got on a land rig in Alberta and came back to
Newfoundland when they had some experience under their belts,
because that's what our people do. Ron wasn't working for a while, a
few months, when ODECO got a rig on the Grand Banks. I knew the
drilling manager and asked him if there was any chance they were
hiring, I had two brothers interested in working offshore. He basically
took them on right there, sight unseen.

I was single at the time, a mother of three young children, and Ron
lived with us before he went out West and moved in again when he
came home. He was a great help with the children and the finances.
It might've seemed kind of strange to an outsider, a brother and sister
living together, but for our family we didn't think anything of it
because we were such good friends. Even when I met my husband,
Wayne, he said that he had never seen a brother and sister coexisting
like that. To him, it was unusual. Ron was in the process of a divorce

then, too—he really struggled with that, and it killed him when the marriage finally ended—that's why he went out West, to get away: the geographical cure. But when he came back and got hired by ODECO, was living in a happy environment, he really felt like he was finally getting his life back on track. He'd even planned for his first vacation. On his calendar, he had the date marked off. He was really excited about that.

My children didn't have much contact with their father, and Ron was absolutely marvellous to them. He filled a void in their lives. One year, my oldest daughter got a bike for her birthday. The next day, the others asked could they get bikes, too? I told them we'd have to see, not right now. When I came home from work, Ron had bikes for both of them.

When he was out there on the rig, Ron quite liked it. The two of them, Ron and Ray, were roustabouts and weren't getting much training. He never mentioned working conditions to me because he would never want me to worry over things that didn't need to be worried over or couldn't be helped.

At the beginning of February, Wayne, who was a geologist with Mobil, came up to me at work and said that the rig had taken a bad list. He knew I went through all the offshore reports before sending them to Calgary, but nothing had come in and it certainly hadn't been talked about in the office. Wayne said, "We have to find out what's going on, if that rig took a list."

Ray was out there then and came in later that day. He confirmed the rumours. "It was utter chaos, nobody knew what to do. If anything happens, anything serious, they won't save a man. I'm telling you everyone will die."

I told him he was cracked.

But there were some problems, I knew that. Mobil had sent out a new drilling supervisor that February. He was from Nova Scotia and had previously worked on *Sedco 706*. He was a seasoned guy, older, a cool guy, too, and they asked him to go out to the *Ranger* and give them his assessment. It was apparent to me then that communication between the rig and the office was terrible. It was the attitude of indifference by the company and its managers. Drill, drill, drill. Make money. That was the bottom line. We don't want any excuses, just keep drilling.

A few days after all of that, Ron went back out. Wayne drove him to the heliport that last time. He told me later that Ron didn't want to go offshore because of the stormy weather. He said, "Let's turn around and forget about this." That still haunts me.

On Monday, one of the girls I worked with came to my house. She knew Ron quite well. It was very early, still dark. "Elaine, I thought someone should tell you that the *Ranger* is in serious trouble." She didn't know much else.

The storm of the previous evening had just started to taper off. I've heard other people who had loved ones on the rig say they couldn't sleep, that they had terrible dreams. It sounds a bit naïve, but what was going on out on the *Ranger* never entered my mind. It was like the *Titanic*. ODECO told us it was the biggest and the best, and everybody believed them.

I called Wayne at work and told him I was coming down. "No, I don't want you to do that," he said. "I want you to go with your parents."

I was emphatic. "I work with the drilling manager and I know these things inside and out. They'll need my help."

Having no idea of what had happened, I went in. There was pandemonium at the Mobil office. All of the employees were there. Phones were ringing off the hooks. They were trying desperately to set up an emergency response team.

Not too long after I arrived, Merv Graham asked me to take notes. "We're in contact with helicopters flying over the site."

I had no idea the rig was lost. I knew it was in trouble, that they were abandoning ship—that's it. I figured Ron was all right because he hated the water, that he wouldn't leave the rig. No one corrected me. Maybe people just couldn't come out and say it. Even Wayne couldn't tell me, because he knew how much Ron meant to me.

What came over the radio was gruesome and frightening. The helicopters could find no signs of life. Bodies were floating downturned in the water with no survival suits on.

That's when I lost it, because then I knew. Wayne had to call Ray to come get me.

I went home with my parents.

I never understood why Merv Graham asked me to take notes, knowing I had a brother out there. He had already received radio transmissions, already knew what was going on, that the rig had sunk. Maybe he was in such a fog that he didn't realize. Maybe his mind was racing like everyone else's and he just wasn't thinking.

I spent a lot of time at my parent's house waiting for word, hoping. Calls started to come in from legal firms in the United States wanting to represent us. At that point, it didn't even occur to us that people would be suing, that there'd be lawsuits against the companies. You're just so devastated you don't think like that. I told them we weren't interested.

After about a week, our family had pretty much given up hope. I was with Wayne and the kids at my house on Reid Street when he finally got the call. He said that he had to go out for a little while and didn't make much of it. Dad and Ray dropped by and they were just leaving when Wayne pulled up. I looked out because I didn't know who it was. He waved them down and went to talk to them. I knew something was going on. Then Dad got out of his car and they came back into the house. That's when Wayne told us, they had Ron's body. It came out later that the supply vessels almost got people in a lifeboat. Apparently, Ron was amongst those still strapped in. I often think of how close they came to saving him.

Until you had concrete evidence, a body, in the back of your mind you think some miracle is going to happen, that they're still alive somewhere. But I guess that finding him was all God could give us.

Still, every part of me, every part of us, went numb. I was in shock.

There's little in my memory of the children during the next week, or much of anything else—I just couldn't absorb stuff. In fact, for a long while, I had no recollection that my son had had chicken pox. Wayne reminded me years later. One instance that sticks out was at the wake. There was this poor old lady in the next room who was from St. Patrick's Mercy Home. The room was totally empty, and my youngest, always precocious, wandered in. She came back where we all were and said, "There's an old woman out in the next room. Was she on the rig, too?" That gave a little bit of comic relief. Ron would've certainly appreciated that, coming from one of the kids.

His death was very hard on Ray. Through it all, I remember him trying to be really strong because they were so close. They both left and drove out to Calgary and spent a year there and then drove back. They were best buddies. It was around the time of the funeral, we were at my parents' house, and he kind of went off by himself and broke down. He said he wasn't going to do it to himself, but he had to, he had to let his emotions out. Ray left a little while after that and went to work on a rig off the coast of Brazil. He didn't stay very long. It was too close to when the *Ranger* went down, and he quit and got out of the oil industry altogether.

I took the next week off but had to eventually go back to work. After about eight months down there, things started to return to normal. During that time, I didn't really exist, because I didn't like what was going on. It was a horrible environment. I was privy to many things the other families weren't, and it appeared to me that they were trying to make it seem as though the disaster wasn't their fault. There was this rumour going around that the inexperience of the Newfoundlanders on board was to blame, that they didn't know what they were doing. There were other comments I heard from people in the oil industry, things like we're all fishermen, we're used to tragedy at sea. I started to think that they were trying to ease their own conscience because there'd been problems and not one of them had done anything to fix them. They even got rid of the management here in town. It was all done very quickly.

At the same time, I was a member of the *Ocean Ranger* Families Foundation who was putting serious pressure on Mobil and the government to change offshore safety. I wanted to do something, to help, and I felt that with my background in the oil industry I could offer some assistance. At first, it was a bit odd, because I thought it might mean my job. But I soon realized that they couldn't fire me—they didn't want the bad press, didn't want such a messy situation getting out.

Some of the people at Mobil were very sincere. A month after the *Ranger* sank the President, Bill Mason, was down from Calgary and stopped by my desk. I could tell he was quite stricken. In my mind, he was not a typical oil person, he was a gentleman. He said, "Elaine, I'm so sorry to hear about the loss of your brother." The following February, I was working for the drilling superintendant, and he's new, hadn't been there when the *Ranger* went down. "Take the fifteenth off," he said. "It isn't necessary for you to come in." I thought that was pretty decent.

I continued to work directly for Mobil until just a few years ago. There were a lot of times when I had to bite my tongue. I really wanted to quit, didn't want to be there. What upset me most was when the anniversary would come around and the PR machine would roll out. Their image was the focus, not the human cost. I stayed there because I knew Ron was a realist and practical. I was single with three young children—I had to stick it out.

On one of the anniversaries, I remember the headline on the front page of *The Evening Telegram*. It talked about the cost of oil and that we've already paid too high a price for prosperity. It was certainly too high for me and my family. The whole thing, losing Ron like that, still leaves me raw. But I guess it will always be emotional, because it affected so many people, so many families. It was just such a horrible thing.

Then there's the guilt, the guilt of being instrumental in getting Ron the job. If it had been one of my other siblings, I would've been just as upset, but he and I had a particular closeness, a unique bond. I carried around that guilt for a long, long time.

In letters from the mainland, Ron Foley often called his daughter, Connie, "My darling."

A MONOLOGUE ABOUT SEEING HIM THAT LAST TIME
Connie, a daughter

I don't really remember the storm. I do remember finding out about the rig. I was staying at a friend's house and her mom came up to get me out of bed. It was only seven o'clock in the morning but it was already all over the radio and the television. Reports were coming in that the *Ocean Ranger* was in trouble and that the men had taken to the lifeboats. I figured Dad would be home soon and rushed out the door because the basement apartment we shared on Logy Bay Road was in a bit of a state. I wanted it tidy before he got in.

Aunt Helen came down to see how I was doing. She was the youngest of Dad's siblings and they were very close. She even lived with us for a time. I was focused on cleaning and didn't want to deal with whatever she was trying to say because it was just too hard to conceive of. At some point, watching the news, standing with a broom in my hand, the realization struck me: *He's not coming back.*

I was nineteen, the oldest of five. He was forty-seven and divorced from my mother.

We had just started living together when he decided to go out to Alberta in search of work on the land rigs. When he came home, he got a job with ODECO as a roustabout.

That was a year before he died.

At the time, I was an immature teenager who didn't know where her head was, where she was going or how she was going to get there. I had a job at the Taxation Centre while I did typing at night, trying to get a little bit of education and experience. Then I got a part-time job at Zellers.

I depended on Dad quite a bit. Everyone depended on him, especially Mom and my brothers and sisters, and he did everything he could for us. Although he had only Grade 6, he worked all his life and did what he had to do to make a dollar. I can only imagine how hard he worked out there.

He rarely mentioned his experiences on the rig. I guess he didn't want me worrying. He never sat me down and told me exactly what was going on out there, but I got the feeling it wasn't the safest place in the world. He did tell me he almost fell off once. One of his close friends, Michael Maurice, was out there with him. They were working next to the railing and he fell over, toppled out over the side. Michael just reached out and caught the cuff of his pants. Dad said that as he hung there upside down for God only knows how long he could see the water washing up over the pontoons eighty feet below.

I can still see him going through the door that final time. It's like a movie running through my mind. Standing in the porch, he had his hand on the knob and I went and put my arms around his neck, kissed him and told him I loved him. He was so surprised. We were never the type to hug and kiss, and I often ask myself, *What made me do that?*

I count myself very lucky. A lot of people didn't get that opportunity.

That whole week was like a rollercoaster going up and down, trying to find some information, any information. I would call the Mobil and ODECO offices and they wouldn't tell us anything. Dad had a large family—there were seven of them—and they were with me. Mom came out with my brothers and sister. We had our hopes up that maybe there was a part of the rig where they could've gone, that if someone got to them they might be saved.

I prayed.

Around mid-week, I was sitting on the couch watching *ASN News*—they still had captioned programming for the hard of hearing—when the words scrolled up the screen that there were no survivors. Then we knew for sure.

It was so traumatic. I would cry and cry and then go to bed totally exhausted and close my eyes, but as soon as I opened them up reality would hit me right in the face. That week I lost twenty pounds.

At the ecumenical service, there was a massive turnout. Walking up to the front of the Basilica, I saw Premier Peckford sitting in the front pew with other government officials. I thought, *What are they doing up here when we have to sit in the back? I guess you're more important, the news and the media are more important than us, the families.* For such a solemn occasion, it put a really bad taste in my mouth.

A few days later, we got a call at my apartment. They had recovered a body thought to be Dad's and wanted me to make the positive identification. There was no way I could do that. Uncles Bernard and Amberse were there and they went instead. When they got back, it was obvious they were completely overwhelmed by the experience. I had to go to the ODECO office to pick up the few things found in his pockets: a waterlogged pack of cigarettes, a watch that was stopped at four o'clock, some matches and a pocket knife. It was then that I learned he was found with a life jacket on.

He was buried through St. Patrick's. My brothers and sisters were all there with me, and Mom was, too, because she wanted to support her children. But it was Dad's family and she really felt like she had to keep to the background as best she could. That must've been so hard for her.

Everyone was talking about lawyers, and the family knew we had to sue. We were already receiving Worker's Compensation, and the first thing we found out was that we had to pay it all back before we could proceed. I went to Dad's lawyer, but within a few days my cousin recommended his, who happened to be representing a number of other families.

Being the oldest child, I had to deal with all the legal concerns. That was probably not the best choice, but the only one we had.

I think I grew up pretty fast then.

My brother Tim moved in with me for the short time I continued to rent the basement apartment. *The Evening Telegram* started accepting donations on behalf of the families, and I went a few times to get $100 for food. I guess they didn't know me from Adam, and I was treated with suspicion. Then my brother Sean came out and found a job but needed a car to get back and forth. I went down again looking for a few hundred dollars to help him out. I only spoke to a secretary. "My boss would like to know what you're going to do with the money."

People had donated so much out of the kindness of their hearts, people who probably had less than us, and yet we were seeing so little of it. I was livid. "My darling, if my father wasn't dead, I wouldn't have to ask you for money!"

Mom was totally cut off. Up until Dad died, she was receiving child support, but then had nothing. Because my parents were divorced, she couldn't file for compensation or sue the companies. She had two youngsters still in school, and I tried to help her out as best I could. But I was making only minimum wage. Nobody ever called to ask if her children had shoes on their feet or food in their bellies. Nobody.

Dad's insurance money was barely enough to buy a trailer. My mortgage was minimal, but I often had no food to eat or oil in the furnace, and the three of us were frozen most of the time. At least we had a roof over our heads, and I'm sure I wasn't the only one who didn't have money to get the bus to work or who lived on eggs and bologna sandwiches.

When the settlement finally came through, I was an adult. I was no longer a dependant and entitled to nothing. The lawyers representing all of Dad's kids were given a lump sum to spread out. They came up with a formula based on need and age. When I went to sign off on the papers as Dad's next-of-kin, they told me they were giving me $9,000 which they had skimmed off what was going to my brothers and sisters. Not like I didn't need it. I had a few thousand dollars left to pay on the trailer, and I bought a washer and dryer and a bed out of what remained. The money didn't last long.

I went along with whatever the lawyers suggested because I didn't understand anything. I didn't know how to look for information or what questions to ask, never knew what was best for my father's children, for us, and made some bad decisions.

Now, at forty-five, if this happened to me again today, it would be different.

Gerald Power at the Torbay hangar. Sandra, his partner, drove him to the heliport that last time, a week before the rig sank.

A MONOLOGUE ABOUT AN ABSOLUTE VOID
Sandra, a partner

I don't know a lot about Gerald growing up because I didn't meet him until he was almost thirty. He was from a large Catholic family and went to Gonzaga. As a young man, he left for British Columbia in search of work, and when all the talk of oil started up in the province he figured he could make a good life for himself here and returned home.

I met him in September 1979. We were out with some mutual friends and happened to strike up a conversation. At first, I didn't know how to take him because he was so very quiet, but he eventually opened up and talked about the drill ship he worked on off the coast of India and his hopes of getting a job on the oil patch. He was leaving for four weeks but asked if he could call me when he got back. Sure enough, he did, and we went out on our first date in December.

We were soon an item and had a lot of fun together going to house parties and barbeques and driving around listening to Bob Seger. We started to see more of one another and our relationship soon became a steady thing.

I was working at the Janeway Hospital as a secretary. Gerald had been gone for six weeks, his last hitch aboard that particular ship, and I remember as soon he got home he came down to see me. He was very excited. He had just gotten a job on a new rig that was going to drill on the Grand Banks. It was supposed to be the biggest semi-submersible in the world, the *Ocean Ranger*. He was going to start soon, he explained, and the money would be great.

I had no contact with Gerald during his three weeks on the rig or for the first few days when he came in and he went off with his buddies. Although I missed him dearly, he seemed to enjoy his new job. Besides, we spent most of his time off together, and I quickly became used to that way of life.

In 1981, I became pregnant.

We often talked about what we were going to do, our future together, and figured it best for him to stay on the rig for the time being. He had just received a promotion to assistant crane operator, and we discussed building a house somewhere in St. John's, or maybe Outer Cove, in late spring. The baby would be born then, and we would become a family and eventually get married.

Gerald never spoke much about life on the rig, maybe because I was pregnant and he didn't want me to worry. But I knew it was pretty rough out there, that the safety drills and exercises were a joke. Once, late at night, he said if anything should ever happen out there that he would go down into the air chamber. I never thought much of it because he felt safe aboard the *Ranger*. It was the trip out in the chopper that made him nervous.

The Tuesday before the rig sank, I drove Gerald to the heliport, and I'm glad. He didn't want to go out because he had hurt his leg and made the decision at the last minute. Before he got out of the car, he said, "The next time I come in you'll have the baby." My final memory of Gerald is of him walking off towards the hangar, the sun just coming up over the horizon. Then, he was gone.

It was quite stormy on Valentine's Day, and my sister sent her boyfriend to come get my daughter and I in his truck. The snow was so high it was piled up past the door, and we had to crawl out through a window. We went to my mother's and I slept for most of the day, not having an inkling of what was about to transpire. That night, I got up to use the bathroom. My father was standing by the kitchen window looking out. He commented on how stormy the weather was and said he'd spoken to his sister—she lived by the ocean—and that the way in which the wind was hitting her house was nothing like she had ever experienced before. Then, again, sometime early in the morning, I woke and sat straight up in bed. I felt anxious, but didn't know why.

I was eating breakfast with my daughter when my mother said the *Ocean Ranger* was in trouble and men were in the water. We turned on the radio. At that point, the reports hadn't indicated the rig was actually gone, just that it'd dropped off the radar. I assumed they would bring the crew in soon and looked forward to Gerald coming home early. We waited to see the helicopters, but by eleven o'clock we knew there were no survivors. We knew everyone was gone.

Time seemed to drag on for an eternity. It was on the news the whole morning, the top story, and we waited for word from the company but heard nothing. We were constantly in contact with Gerald's family, but they didn't know anything, either. ODECO wasn't giving out information and their doors were locked. Even the media couldn't get through.

That evening, I was alone in the living room and the back door blew open. A chill then came over me which went right down my side. I'll never experience that kind of cold again. I think Gerald died then, at around seven o'clock, because he went into that air chamber and never got in a lifeboat. He told me they had twenty-four hours worth of air down there. I think he lived until then.

Shortly thereafter, Gerald's older brother came over with his two daughters. He said that the parish priest and the police had been to his parents' house to inform them that all hands aboard the rig were lost. Everyone started crying—his nieces, my mother. I couldn't cry. My baby was moving a lot, but after that not so much, and I was more than a bit concerned. I had to try and stay calm.

The next week everyone went numb. We were all filled with sadness and disbelief. I spent quite a bit of time at Gerald's parents' house hoping he would be found. I watched the news reports of the supply vessels bringing bodies in, and even went down to the harbour when I heard they found eight or nine men. But his was never recovered.

His family held a funeral mass. I didn't go because I was under a lot of stress and had to think about the baby. I remember standing in my kitchen window watching the procession go by. It was a very lonely time for me, not knowing what the future held, but unwilling to think that far ahead.

Two weeks later, I gave birth.

During a routine check-up, my physician told me he could detect *two* heartbeats. He didn't want any surprises and he sent me for an ultrasound. It showed I was expecting twins. Of course, Gerald never knew we were going to have twins, and neither did I. They were born on March 1—one at 8:44 in the evening and the other at 8:47—the day their father would have finished his hitch, had he lived. I named them Matthew and Tim. They were so much like their father, especially Matthew. I've often heard people who knew Gerald as a youngster say he'd never be dead as long as those boys are alive.

I was something of a celebrity at the hospital. I had a private room and all the staff knew I had lost my partner on the *Ocean Ranger*. They didn't talk to me all that much, probably because they didn't know what to say. But their few words of comfort helped a great deal.

Gerald was very much on my mind, and I imagined I saw him everywhere. It was the trauma of losing so much, losing Gerald, losing everything that was yet to come. One night I woke and there was a male nurse standing in the doorway. I thought it was him. It wasn't until he spoke that I realized it wasn't. When I was released from the hospital, I was driving down to Outer Cover to visit Gerald's sister. There's a stretch between the town hall and the hill and there was a guy walking up the road, and I thought for sure it was Gerald—the way he walked, his clothes, everything about him put me in mind of him. I was just so sure.

Even with the support of our families and the community, it was difficult bringing the boys up alone. I was overwhelmed most of the time and a real emotional wreck. I couldn't eat or sleep and didn't want to leave the house. I withdrew into myself. I had a daughter in kindergarten, there were the twins, and I went back to work that summer because there was no money coming in. We didn't get any kind of a settlement until 1983, and even then I had to go to court to determine that the boys were Gerald's children.

Growing up, the boys missed having a father in their lives and never knew what it was like to have one. That's the saddest part. It's not the same when you marry someone else. They might accept the boys as their own, but they're not flesh and blood. When they were at school and went to hockey, I was there cheering for them, supporting them. Father's Day was always hard. They would make a card for their poppy, but then he died when they were seven, leaving an absolute void in their lives.

Because Gerald and I were together for a few years and planned a life together, I often think of what it would have been like had he lived. Things certainly would have been different. We talk about that a lot. I know he would have been proud of his sons. They're wonderful boys, and they miss him.

A MONOLOGUE ABOUT THE NEXT ONE TO GO
Tracey, a daughter

With four kids and a wife at home and having to live paycheque to paycheque, Dad did whatever he could to support his family. Among other things, he drove a taxi. One of his regulars knew he was handy in the kitchen and told him of an opportunity coming up with Atlantic Fortier as a cook offshore. Dad didn't have his papers but went down anyway, found out the guy doing the hiring was a friend of his, and ended up getting the job. For the next six months—until his death—he worked on the *Ocean Ranger*.

The extra money was great, and we began to live a little outside of our means. There were always certain things we could never afford. We often ate fish simply because it was the cheapest thing available, but soon started buying chicken and turkey and steak. We never had new toys, either; they were always hand-me-downs. With his first cheque, Dad bought my sister a new bike. That was a real big deal. We even got a car, an old Pontiac, because he was determined to teach Mom how to drive. I still remember how short she seemed behind the wheel.

A lot of the guys Dad knew went off with their buddies when they got in. He had a family, didn't like the long stretches offshore, and always made up for being away. We used to spend a lot of time at my grandparents' house, and Mom and Dad would have their date nights. With us, he'd bake sweets. Once, he tried making ladyfingers, but screwed them up so bad they came out as these giant cookies we called "Monster Cookies." From then on, he made them as our special little treat.

I don't know much about his experiences working on the rig, but he seemed to enjoy it. He got along with most of the guys and even made some very good friends. I do remember he got locked in the freezer. There was a buzzer on the inside, but his boss thought the fire alarm had gone off and left him. He ended up coming home with pneumonia. One story has stayed with me more than any other. For a while, Dad was a crossing guard and got to know Dana Bradley as she walked back and forth from school. He happened to be off his hitch when she was murdered. He told us he suspected a guy on the *Ranger* had done it. "There's just something strange about this guy," he said. "He doesn't ring true with me." According to Dad, he fit the description given to police, sold his car soon after her body was discovered near Maddox Cove, and even hid away the few times the police were out to the rig. I figure maybe the reason why they've never solved the case is that he died with the rest of the men.

A week before the rig sank, Dad got shore leave to come in for his grandfather's funeral. He seemed overly anxious, held Mom's hand too tight on the drive to Hant's Harbour, and even read the Bible from cover to cover, something he'd never done before in his life. Then, when they were carrying the casket to the gravesite, he almost fell in, and a few of his cousins started tormenting him that he'd be the next to go. That was February 8. Years later, I spoke to an old friend of his. Dad told him about the list of the previous Saturday and that no one was safe on the rig, that he wished he never had to go back out but knew he had to put his fears to rest if he was to provide a better life for his family.

The night of the storm, the four of us were kept awake because we were worried about him. Mom tried to tuck us in but I was crying, and my younger brother crawled in with me. She said the *Ocean Ranger* was a big rig, that the men would batten down and they'd be just fine. But the storm was getting heavier and heavier, and I couldn't sleep.

The next morning, we heard the rig had sent out a mayday. Mom wasn't too sure what that meant, and a friend who had dropped by to see how she was doing said it was probably nothing, that they just wanted to let the onshore office know they were okay but that they needed to evacuate everyone. It seemed to bring her some small measure of relief.

Things were not as they seemed. Because they thought it would be easier for a friend to break the news to her, the company called our neighbour to inform them that the rig had sunk and that there were no survivors.

Mom went as white as a sheet. Somehow, she managed to drag us all into the living room, sat us down and took my brother up on her lap. "I've got some news to tell you, and I don't want you to hear it from the radio or the television or a friend from school. You're going to hear it from me. Your father is gone."

I called her down to the dirt. I said everything to her I could possibly think of and ran out the door and didn't come home for hours. For weeks afterwards, I wouldn't even look at her. There was no way I would accept that he was gone. When they found a lifeboat, I thought that he might be in it. When twenty-two bodies were recovered, I asked if one of them was his. "No," she said. "He's not coming home."

The saddest part of it all was the memorial service held at St. James United Church on University Avenue. When they called out the eighty-four names, my grandmother started crying and eventually collapsed. An ambulance had to be called. I kept repeating, "You did this, Daddy—you did. This is all because of you." That's as vivid in my mind as if it was yesterday. It was the only time in my life when I hated my father.

Shortly thereafter, we moved. I was angry because if he was alive somewhere he was going to come home, but now he'd never be able to find us.

Mom did her best raising us. She looked for a job but with little education was left with few options. She was a crossing guard, a secretary, and even worked in a school cafeteria—anything to put food on our table and a roof above our heads. If she had a driver's license I'm sure she would've been taxiing. It was so hard on her losing the love of her life and then having to go on without him while trying to raise four children all under the age of twelve. I don't think she ever got over losing him. We took it day by day and learned to cope.

When Cle Newhook and Lorraine Michael started the *Ocean Ranger* Families Foundation, Mom became actively involved. They said the public deserved to know what had happened, and that the companies should take responsibility for the loss of life. At the time, Mom blamed everybody for his death: the company that Dad worked for because they hadn't had any of them insured, Mobil for sending them out, and ODECO for making the rig in the first place. She eventually became something of a secretary for the Families Foundation. She was the one who sat in the courtroom when witnesses described what had happened. She was the one who took down all the notes and minutes. She volunteered to do those things, not because she wanted to, but because she had to. It gave her some piece of mind knowing she wasn't just sitting idly by. At first, she made it a point to say, "You're going to be curious about things, and you're going to want to know." Every day there was some new development and we were first to hear about it.

RIG   MIKE HEFFERNAN

The only thing she didn't tell us was how Dad died. I often wished she had because it left us assuming. For years, I thought he suffered. Once I found out he died of hypothermia, that he died relatively painless and quick, I found myself at ease.

Things did get better for us, but they could never be the same. Mom remarried and it was nice to have a father figure around. Although she wanted to pursue it further, she had her children to think of, and she agreed to the settlement reached between the families and the companies. It wasn't as tough financially, but we always felt that it was blood money.

When you're young, it's painful losing your father. You see dads with their kids and a lot of things run through your mind: *Why can't my daddy be here doing this with me? Why did he have to die on the rig?* You blame him while at the same time you're too young to really understand why he isn't there to see you grow up. It was especially hard on my brother because he was so young and really didn't know him. He should've had that opportunity.

Every February 15, I think, *This is the big one. How do I get through this day?* My brother and I attend the memorial service. We won't go up to the plaque with everyone else, we'll throw some flowers into the ocean and say a little prayer and talk to him instead. Mom used to go but doesn't anymore. It's too painful for her. Besides a few funny stories, she no longer talks about my father. My sisters don't go, either—I think they want to leave the past behind them.

The pain of having lost him never really heals, and I'm not sure if it gets easier or harder as time goes on. There are certain years that it's as fresh as ever and some that are not so bad. Most times it seems like it just happened.

Dad was just thirty-two when he died and still very young. He was so kind and funny and generous and such a wonderful father. I often wonder why he can't still be here with us.

Poet and aspiring journalist, Greg Tiller. Many of his poems were put to music using this guitar.

A MONOLOGUE ABOUT BEING PROUD OF YOUR SON
Evelyn, a mother

had two daughters but wanted a son so badly. Then I had Greg. He was a loving person and a good boy all through school. The only time he ever got in trouble was for once using foul language in French class. I was so shocked when that happened because I didn't think he even knew those words. His teachers would often say something happened between his brain and his hands and that he didn't work hard enough. As his mother, I thought he was just perfect.

Greg was quite smart and very artistic—there's no doubt about that. In his bedroom down in the basement, he wrote poetry and sometimes put his words to music. I don't know how good his writing really was because he never got the chance to rewrite much of it.

His father worked in Labrador. It's strange, but I always felt that as long as he provided for his children, his being away from us all the time was alright. Although Greg visited him several times, treated him with respect, he resented not having him around, and I could see a certain detachment there. Maybe that's why he was so protective and honest and never wanted me to worry.

After finishing high school, Greg didn't know what he wanted to do with his life. For a while, he had a number of odd jobs and even sold vacuum cleaners. I think he lasted at that for a day. A friend of mine said he could get him a job out West with Porta Test Systems, which would have something to do with testing the quantity and quality of crude oil. Greg left his car and flew up to Alberta. I often spoke to him on the phone, and I knew that spending a lot of time in motels made him lonely because he had left behind a girlfriend.

He was out there for about six months, came home to work on *Sedco 706* and then got a job on the *Ocean Ranger*. In comparison to what his friends were making, his salary was substantial. Although he wasn't materialistic, like most boys his age, he didn't have much trouble spending money and soon bought a car. The Celica was used and not top-notch, but a good car for the time—very sporty. Before that, he had a Datsun, which was a real heap of junk, and then there was the hatchback he used to sell vacuum cleaners out of. I remember Greg came home and said what a rotten piece of junk he'd just bought and he was going to spread the word that the dealer had ripped him off. He asked, "Is that blackmail?" I laughed.

Greg didn't like working on the rig; towards the end, I could see something of a change in him. Several times he mentioned a few things in passing, that it was rough work out there, but never anything specific. He was very close with his sister Karen and they talked a lot. His supervisors reprimanded him once because they wanted him to flush the deck with water. He refused and was sent in. I guess he was trained a certain way, felt that the procedure with which he was familiar was the safest, and that whoever was giving him orders didn't know what they were talking about. He thought he was doing the right thing.

That was supposed to be his last trip out. He had registered for the spring semester and was accepted into university as a journalism student.

Barely home a week, he told me he had to go back. I recall it so plainly. I asked him why, and he explained that something had gone wrong with the well and that they were in need of a few extra men. I'm not sure how accurate that is, but it's what he told me, and it's my truth. I didn't know there had been a list on the rig, and neither did Greg. He shouldn't have gone out.

When we got up that morning, it was snowing. Not having much confidence in my driving, Greg said, "Mom, I don't want you to drive me to the airport. It's too stormy." He got one of his buddies to drop him off instead. That's the kind of son he was.

A week later, at about seven o'clock in the morning, my daughter, Maxine, was getting ready for university when the phone rang. It was the company—the rig was in trouble. They continued to call but couldn't give us any additional information. All day I wondered if they would be picked up and rescued. By that evening, we knew he was gone.

I kept thinking of how scared he must've been, but that he would've gone along with the rest of them: *This is it. It has to be this way.* When it's your child, you don't want them to suffer, and I hoped and prayed that he'd been asleep and hadn't known what was going on. I now know he knew. At least the way the weather was that night it would've been quick for them. I tried my best to think those sorts of thoughts.

My daughters found it pretty difficult, especially Karen—they were real buddies—and she just couldn't accept it.

The whole family was here, including Greg's father. Greg's uncle, an RCMP officer from Ottawa, spent a week with us, too. As each ship came into the harbour, he would go down to see if Greg's body was on it, and each time he'd come back to the house and say, "Ours is not there." In the end, it never was.

Karen was down in Greg's room sorting through his things when she came up with his book of poetry. It was something he always took with him, but, for whatever reason, hadn't that last time out. "You know," she said, handing it to her father, "the last poem in there is called 'Rig'." Nobody had heard or seen it before, not even his friends. It talked about Mother Earth taking revenge on us for our misdeeds and greed. The family thought he had somehow foreseen the disaster. I couldn't believe what he had written, that in his heart and soul he knew something dreadful was about to happen.

Max, my then husband, took it to show his lawyer, had it copyrighted, and it was published in *The Evening Telegram, The Herald* and later reprinted in a Language Arts textbook.

I waited months and months for Greg to return. I would go about my housework and then sit staring out the window at the Celica in the driveway. The neighbour across the street said, "It's time you sold that car. You know he's not coming back." I didn't like that one bit. It wasn't until June that Maxine snapped me out of it: "Mom, I don't count at all, do I?" I thought, *My God, I've got to wake up!* I traded in his car on one for my daughter. That night I dreamt of Greg. In it, he came back and told me it was all right that I'd sold his car—he could get a new one. I haven't dreamt of him since.

It wasn't until last summer when I was invited to his high school reunion that I really accepted he was truly gone forever. His classmates paid tribute to five of their friends that had passed away, including Greg, with a video. After that, I could finally admit to myself I would never see my son again. Who knows, maybe I will. I was moved by the fact that he hadn't been forgotten, that he had meant so much to them.

Our family has never forgotten him. How could we? We keep his memory alive on his birthdays, and my daughter comes from

Vancouver every year to attend the memorial service with me. The other children call. For a long time I didn't attend. I got brave after a friend encouraged me: "C'mon, let's do it!" Finally, I did.

I could never go back in Greg's room, or throw out his things. I still have his jackets in the closet, including the leather one with the fur inside, a trunkful of letters, his clothes, his razor—everything. Even his records are still down on the shelves. His sister had to pack it all up. It was only last year that I gave away one of his guitars to his nephew, my grandson. It's sad, but it's just as well while they're still good.

In reading his poetry, I felt that he was very unhappy, which upset me. Because of that I turned down an offer to have it published. I realize now he was just so young and only coming into his own as an artist and didn't have the chance to grow. I often wonder what would have happened had he lived.

I had Greg for twenty-one years, and I'm glad I had him for that short time. I was so proud of him. But I suppose all mothers are proud of their children, aren't they?

High school photo of Craig Tilley. His mother, Patricia, was one of the last family members to reach an out-of-court settlement with the oil companies.

A MONOLOGUE ABOUT STICKING TOGETHER
THROUGH THE WORST OF IT
Patricia, a mother

When Craig was found, he didn't have a mark on him—he was fully clothed and had his hard hat on. What made me so bitter and angry was the fact that he came so close to being a survivor. Imagine Mobil and ODECO with all their billions and trillions of dollars bringing those men out to the rig with no proper survival suits. You couldn't dream that up if you tried.

Our lawyers wanted us to settle, but I wasn't willing to let the oil companies off the hook that easy. Pat Hickey and I sued. We went through the ropes with them.

Craig was my oldest boy but the youngest on the rig. He was nineteen.

In those days, it was a big deal to work offshore, and you had to have a connection to get out there. My brother used to cut Blondie Gernandt's hair, and I took Craig to see him at his office. "Your mother's blonde, you're blonde and I'm blonde," he said. "We'll probably hire you." With absolutely no experience, he got the job.

Being his mother, I went out and got him insulated underwear and warm clothes and everything that he'd need to work on the North Atlantic. But, honestly, I really wasn't aware of how vicious it could get out there.

He left for his first hitch the second week of December. For those twenty-one days, I was scared to death.

I was getting gas at Irving on Torbay Road—we lived next door—when he walked in. I started crying right then and there because I was so happy to see him. He took a rock out of his pocket. "Here, Mom. I'm not supposed to have this, but I thought you'd like a souvenir." It was pure oil.

His first cheque was for $2,400. That was big money then—you're talking twenty-seven years ago. Like most guys his age, he wanted a car. So we went to the bank, financed it, and he was driving around the whole day as proud as a peacock. He had his eye on a girl who was in my brother's barber shop. With the little bit of confidence he got from his new car and his new job, he asked her out. That night was the last time I saw him. He looked so handsome with his hair all done off and a new sweater and white shirt on. "If you weren't my son," I said, "I'd be after you myself."

The next morning, I was still in bed when he yelled out, "I'm on my way." He didn't bother coming up because it was so early and he was in a rush to catch the chopper.

My husband and I were in the country when I turned on the radio at six in the morning. It was Monday. I never listen to the radio and don't usually get up at that hour, but it was such a stormy night that I wasn't sleeping. It was then that I heard the *Ranger* was in serious trouble. "I know Craig's all right because he's in a life jacket. We have to get to the airport—he'll be coming in." I was sure he was going to be there; he was so big and strong that nothing could ever happen to him.

We drove to Torbay and I waited in the car while my husband went into the hangar looking for news. When he got back, he said, "We'll head to the house for a cup of tea and some breakfast." Little did I know he knew there were no survivors. He was just trying to figure out a way to tell me.

As soon as we sat down to eat, the phone rang. It was ODECO. "You knew about the oil rig accident?"

"Yes," I said. "Is everything all right?"

"I'm afraid there's little if any hope of survivors."

That night they confirmed our worst fears: my son was gone.

With everyone around me, I sat and waited and never went to bed because each time I closed my eyes I would see Craig's face.

Thursday morning, Monsignor Lawlor came to the door. "Do you know why I'm here?" he asked. "We have your son's body."

"Oh, thank God!"

Even though he was dead, I knew where he was—I had him. Only twenty-two families got the peace of mind that comes with a burial. Poor Pat Hickey went months and months expecting Greg, her son, to be on the phone. As a mother, she couldn't let go.

For the first year, I wasn't much different. I couldn't bring myself to talk about my son's death, had no intentions of suing and didn't want anything to do with that. I made his father take all his things out of the house. I couldn't look at the news or watch television for fear of seeing something on the *Ranger*. Craig's car was locked up in my brother's garage. After six months, he phoned me. "You've got to take the car. I need the space." They wanted to give it to my daughter, but I couldn't bear to look at it every day. It was sold.

The companies soon disappeared, took cover like a bunch of rats, and my frustrations boiled over. I thought, *Those bastards aren't getting away with this!*

My ex-husband hired a lawyer. I went to his office on Duckworth Street and listened to what he had to say. Immediately, I formed the impression he was only after money.

There was a meeting with all the families. We were sitting at this huge table—Pat was next to me—and as I listened to all the wheeling and dealing going on, I was sickened. What should've been about us getting justice for losing our loved ones had turned into a money racket. I leaned over to Pat: "Are you going to let them off this easy?"

"I really don't want to," she said.

"Well, let's you and me stick together and not sign anything."

We shook hands under the table and agreed not to go ahead with what was arranged.

The next day, my lawyer phoned wanting to know my birthday.

"What for?" I asked.

"I'm getting your cheque made out."

"You're not writing any cheque for me. I didn't agree to anything."

"Everyone agreed," he said. "It's a done deal and you *have* to sign."

"I didn't agree to anything. Until the companies admit they're liable and caused the accident through neglect, it's not a done deal in my eyes."

That night I was working in my beauty shop when a bailiff came in and served me with a summons. For the next two weeks, ODECO and Mobil dragged us through the courts claiming breach of contract. I thought, *They can put me in jail because I just don't care.* They weren't interested in what Pat and I were going through—all they wanted was to put the whole thing to bed. We won by the slightest of margins, enough for us to pursue our case in the United States.

We went to New Orleans twice.

The first time, Pat and I felt they were trying to pull the wool over our eyes. The judge was something else. We sat in her office and the first thing she did was offer us a beer. "I know what you ladies are going through," she said. "My husband recently had a big accident, and we just got the settlement over with. Our life is so different now."

I looked at her and asked, "Is he alive?"

"Oh, yes," she said

I was livid. "Well, my son happens to be dead, and I'm never going to see him again!"

Pat and I started crying, and we walked out.

It was a year before we went down again.

We got a call from the lawyer. He explained that we had to put an end to it because he didn't want to pursue it any further and that no one else would represent us. What was done was done.

This time the judge said what we wanted to hear, and we talked to a company representative who made it clear they were responsible but that the company wouldn't budge. The offer they made was final. After six years, we were at the point of exhaustion, anyway.

"So what do you want to do?" I asked Pat.

"I guess we have no choice."

We settled.

Even then, they got off pretty good.

It was never about money. Pat's son, Greg, was a grown man no longer living at home—he'd taken the job as a radio operator to make enough money to get married—and I was a successful businesswoman. Money was the last thing on our minds, but that's what people made it sound like.

Those who didn't understand could be so heartless. I heard some awful stuff.

I had a white Mercedes which I would park at the front of my beauty shop. A woman who was getting her hair done said to the stylist, "Just look at her driving her dead son's car. How can she do that?" After all Pat and I had been through, after all we'd fought for, that's what we had to listen to.

We wanted the companies to admit to their negligence, which wasn't much different than murder, and to pay for what they'd done, because the only way to get at them was through their wallets. We didn't care about the possibility of us getting nothing. We lost our sons and neither they, nor anyone else, could hurt us more than we'd already been hurt.

Carl Fry (left) on the drill floor of the *Ranger*. When Carl's body wasn't recovered, his mother waited years for him to return home.

GOING QUIET
Don, a brother

After Carl died, the *Ocean Ranger* became a curse word in my family, and offshore oil a taboo subject—it just wasn't spoken of. It's out of respect for my mother. When the rig went down, our loss was so dark, she just couldn't acknowledge it.

Even now, our memories aren't clear, especially my own.

There are five boys and two girls in my family, and all but one went out West. When Carl finished high school, he did a trade in carpentry. Not too sure whether or not he wanted to continue in that field, he soon followed us. For the better part of two years, we worked together in the British Columbia lumber camps, and then on the railroad, and he seemed to enjoy the long days and weeks of manual labour. That's the type of guy he was: hardworking and honest. Although he was nineteen and making good money, he wasn't one to dress fancy or buy new trucks, and would always have money in the bank. While kicking around Edmonton, he got a job on the land rigs.

As Newfoundlanders, after you're out there a few years, you start looking towards having a career, raising a family and settling in. I came home to do a trade, but Carl stayed until 1980.

I'm not too sure how he got a job offshore. My brothers would come home once or twice a year and inquire about who was hiring, file some applications and continue to check up on them from Alberta. My older brother, Bob, may very well have gotten a job and set it up for Carl, because I remember Harvey's Oil were hiring, and he went down to their office on the east end of Water Street and was soon working on a drill ship.

Carl started off as a roughneck. Safety standards in the early-eighties left something to be desired, but for him there wasn't a big difference in working out West and working on the Grand Banks. Drilling was drilling. It might've been a few hitches after he first went out that he got promoted to mudman. Despite the obvious ups and downs, he was advancing and quite liked his work—he was young, he was home and he was making good money.

Early Monday morning, I was on my way to school when I heard a blink on the radio, something about the *Ranger* having a rough night, but never thought much of it. I stopped off to pick up some parts for a car I was working on, and the guy there asked if I'd heard that one of the rigs was listing. I wasn't even sure what that was, and he had to tell me it meant she wasn't trim. It completely left my mind because when you heard the words "*Ocean Ranger*" you immediately thought *unsinkable.*

I wasn't in class very long when a knock came to the door. It was the principal, and he asked for me. "I'm sure you're aware that the *Ocean Ranger* is having problems. I'm to tell you to go home." Then and only then did it hit me like a ton of bricks: something serious has happened out there.

Even then, the family had begun to gather at my mother's house on Raleigh Street. All we knew was that the rig was in trouble. It wasn't until early afternoon that the radio reported it had capsized and people were in the water.

Immediately, the big concern was for my mother. She was beginning to fall apart.

On that first day, we were just trying to digest the severity of the situation, and there was still a lot of hope. For years, Carl had played senior hockey in St. John's with Bishop's College. He was big and strong, and everyone knew you didn't mess with him because he didn't mind putting up his fists and having a racket, and that if you wanted to rough up the team you had to start with him first. When the *Ranger* went down, we all thought if there were only a few survivors, Carl would be one of them. He was rough and tough and whatever it took he'd come out on top. Even when the bodies were coming in and Carl wasn't one of them that didn't matter—he was surviving somewhere. As the days grew longer and the news more grim, that's what we held on to.

While we went with the flow of the other families—grieving and going to the services—in the back of our minds, we knew he was alive. A ship would surely pick him up in the next few days. That's why we didn't have a memorial service: none of us could accept that he was gone.

Even when everything settled, the whole family refused to believe. It's how we coped. I talked to my brothers about how I felt. "I just can't accept it. I just can't..." We were all like that.

Carl and I were only a year apart and very close. I'm the one who used to drive him and one of his buddies out to the airport. Maybe that's why I thought the way I did for such a long time, that someday he'd just show up and walk through the door. Whether it was Florida or Toronto, I'd see him in crowds, or sometimes I'd have myself convinced that through his ordeal he had lost his mind and couldn't find us, or that he was on a deserted island somewhere. It was a fantasy of disbelief.

It took my mother years to live again. I was at home until 1984, and it wasn't hard to tell when she was at her lowest. She went through some agonizing periods of depression. She would come home from work and sit and stare out the window and wait for Carl to come down the driveway. She would even have the door unlocked in case he was going to be late. But deep down inside, she knew nothing could bring her son back.

When the inquiry started up and it all came out about the negligence of the companies, there was a lot of anger and shock. Carl never talked to me about that stuff and had no idea of the big picture, so neither did we. My mother couldn't possibly follow the proceedings. As her children, we tuned out a lot and never talked about it at home.

With no grave, the memorial offered somewhere to sit and remember and keep his memory alive within us, and it was nice to see his name on the plaque with the rest of those guys. On the anniversary, I used to take the kids and lay a wreath, but towards the end found it terribly difficult. Mom and I agreed it was too hard on her, too. February 15 has always been a quiet time for her, but we all go quiet that day. We just want to get through it and don't want to even recognize it because of the pain it causes.

As the years go on, you think about what happened less and less. Kids and marriage take precedence in your life. But sometimes things open up. Whenever there's a death in our family, we like to say that if you keep them in your heart and keep them in your conversations they'll never die. My younger brother has a son Carl, and when his name is mentioned memories flow back.

We'll never forget him.

DRAWING A LINE ACROSS THAT YEAR
Cle Newhook; Executive Administrator,
Ocean Ranger *Families Foundation*

When I came home in August, some things had already begun to happen. Lorraine Michael had put together an organization for the families, something along the lines of the *Alexander Keiland* Foundation in Norway. By early fall, the board of directors were convinced they needed someone full time. I happened to be around, was looking for a job, and was hired as their executive administrator.

My first order of business was to find money, because there simply was none.

I'd had some correspondence with Joey Smallwood and decided to pay him a visit. He was as busy as ever, going around like a spin top, and we started talking about what I was up to. I told him about the foundation and the fact that we were broke. Joey scratched his head, held up his finger and said, "I know just the man to call." He picked up the phone and got connected immediately. "Hello, Jean. I have a young man in front of me—Newhook—a born and bred Newfoundlander. They've just started the *Ocean Ranger* Families Foundation, there's no money, and I want you to put in a contribution. Would that be all right?"

After a brief pause, he put down the phone and said, "Air Nova has a ticket for you. Go to Ottawa and pick up your cheque."

I had no idea who he was talking about; of course, it turned out to be Jean Chretien, the Minister of Energy, Mines and Resources.

That was our first allocation of money: $75,000.

There were just two of us in a little downtown office that someone had donated, me and the secretary, back when people still had secretaries, a mother who had lost her son aboard the rig. As we settled in, most of the families became involved in some way.

I distinctly remember the first time Lorraine invited me to a meeting, a place where the families shared their stories and helped one another heal. We all carry around the image of what a widow looks like, but I just wasn't prepared for what I saw when I walked into that room. The women that were there, excluding the parents, were so very young. Most of the guys that died were just kids, just starting their careers, and their wives were girls. I was absolutely floored.

There are no rules about how to grieve, no handbook. But the foundation was certainly a safe haven for them. It's not fair to tell any stories or name any names, but one of the common issues amongst those young widows was the ways in which they were grieving. Every night, one of them would hear her husband come in through the front door and walk up the stairs. She became petrified of it. Her question to me was, *Is this normal?*

In those early days, there was a frenzy to help the families. People wanted to do something concrete. Local business and *The Evening Telegram* set up a mechanism for the public to donate money. While that was going on, the foundation was trying to be born and it had none. Newfoundlanders are generous by nature and a substantial amount was collected. After we started asking questions about what was going to happen to the money, the problem became trying to determine who would receive it. In the end, *The Evening Telegram* devised a kind of litmus test of the most deserving cases. There was a lot of discomfort about that. It was an unfortunate set of circumstances where the right hand wasn't talking to the left. If everyone had sat down together there wouldn't have been that division. But it's easy to rewrite history. Eventually, what remained went into a scholarship fund, which is now administered by a committee within the university.

One of the great frustrations for so many of the families was the facelessness of the people responsible for the accident, the companies. For them, getting to see these people in court was pretty important, to look them in the eye and hear them answer for what they'd let happen. Nobody got there, nobody. With both American and Canadian lawyers involved, and issues arising out of Worker's Compensation—could there be a claim, could there not be a claim—it was a fairly complicated piece of business. I think it's fair to say that a lot of families didn't understand the complexities of what was going on. Although a few tried valiantly to hold out, everyone settled out of court, partly through fatigue and partly through the mystery that were the negotiations between the lawyers.

The Royal Commission was some consolation. The families were there every day, day in and day out, listening to the evidence unfold, as was I. They insisted on being there. I think it was part of the whole healing process, especially for those that never had a body. It's where they did their grieving—in public, for the whole province to see.

Then the most extraordinary thing happened, and it happened very quickly. The families started to turn their attention towards what was happening out there, the offshore, and became preoccupied with making it a safer workplace. Because they had lost so much, nobody, absolutely nobody, could look a woman in the face who'd lost her young son, a wife who'd lost her husband, and tell her to shut up. The foundation lobbied government pretty hard, got up the noses of the oil industry, and we even went to Ottawa to offer some insight for those drafting new Federal safety legislation.

With nowhere to take their stories, a lot of offshore workers came to us. What you have to remember is that this whole industry was imported from the deep south of the United States where the average worker was the helmeted, steel-toed tough guy: a roughneck. It was the kind of industry where men were men and any talk of safety was regarded as soft. That was the culture that existed on the Grand Banks. We accepted whatever those guys had to say and retold their stories in the press, stories about the lack of safety that was still glaringly apparent years after the *Ranger* had sunk.

The issue of how to abandon these rigs wasn't resolved, either. Government was part of the problem, not the solution. For them, the priority was getting oil out of the ground, selling it and making a profit. The technology in use was basically adopted from ships: lifeboats and davits. But a rig is a very different thing—it's an industrial installation. Right from the beginning, we were asking, *Is this the best we can do? We can retrieve people from space, but we can't get them off a rig?* The answer seemed to be that there was no great will to do anything about it. Pure and simple.

After a while, most everyone became tired of listening to us, and it was a real lesson in how communities respond to disasters over the long term. No question, Newfoundland was shaken to its roots by the sinking of the *Ocean Ranger*. The government had us convinced that the oil industry was the miracle cure and the start of a new era. We had this piece of technology out there, a veritable fortress, the unsinkable rig, but then it sank and all these people died. In a cultural sense, so did our dream.

But the disaster was history, it was done, and everyone wanted to draw a line across that year and leave it in the past as a bad memory.

I think it was the money that did it. The public simply weren't able to come to terms with the fact that the wives and the parents and the children were kind of paid off by the companies. One example comes to mind. I was lined up in the bank, and one of the *Ocean Ranger* widows, as they were collectively known, was in front of me. Then, from somewhere behind me, I heard, "Look at that one. She got all her money on the back of her dead husband."

Overnight, our funding just dried up, and we dwindled away.

I've heard it said that some of the improvements made in offshore safety came about as a direct result of the *Ocean Ranger* experience. I don't know. For me, the fact that the families were able to meet and share their stories was the greatest benefit of the foundation, its best service. The rest of the stuff is hard to evaluate. The jury's still out on that one.

PART 5

A SMALL MEASURE OF COMFORT

We carry the dead with us.
　　　　　　　　　 – John Bannville, *The Sea*

The *Ocean Ranger* Memorial under construction. The comprehensive site was designed to nurture two contrasting feelings, exposure to the elements and solace.

A MONOLOGUE ABOUT A GRATIFYING FEELING
Robert Strong; President, Oilfield Technical Society

For the half-dozen or so who put it together—Grace Hughes, Valerie Freeman and a whole bunch of us—the *Ocean Ranger* Memorial became a very special thing in our lives. Although it took three years to find the money and the right architect—and it wasn't fun—it was personally gratifying for us as Newfoundlanders who had lost so many friends.

Crosbie Offshore was quite the empire. With the price of oil $33 a barrel and going to $80, and the Federal Government committing eight billion dollars to frontier development, so much so that 80% of your costs were subsided, it was a logical step for Andrew Crosbie to get involved in the offshore. At their height, they had eight or nine service boats and a host of other companies supplying catering and crews to the rigs. They were the big game in town.

I had corner stores on Springdale Street and Blackmarsh Road and an undergraduate degree in Political Science, which took me the better part of ten years to complete. I was losing money slicing bologna and asked a friend who was a senior manager with Crosbie Offshore how I could possibly get a job in the oil business. "Things are happening," he said. "Put together a resume." Because mine was anything but impressive, I got letters from several local politicians which talked about my knowledge of the local business community and politics. Truth be told, I knew as much about the offshore as I did nuclear physics.

A few months later, I had a company car and a secretary and was making three times what I was on my own.

That company did so much for me, took me in. One day I was selling groceries, and the next, building oil rigs. But I wasn't the only one. There's a load of us who started off with Crosbie Offshore.

I stayed with them until 1986.

The week before the *Ranger* sank, I was in Calgary for a meeting with Chevron, and then went to Ottawa in the hopes of further stimulating the development of offshore Labrador. My wife was at a Vickers and Tarts party with some other women whose husbands were also involved in the industry, one of whom was on the *Ranger*. Thinking

188

back, I gather the girls were talking about how this new industry was something else, how a lot of guys were building careers and making good money while they were at it.

Monday morning, I received a call from the office. "Rob, do you know anyone on the *Ranger*?" Of course, I did—everyone knew someone on the rigs, especially here in St. John's. They told me it'd dropped off the radar around three in the morning, but that no one knew anything else. The House of Commons sat that day and had a minute of silence. I knew then that it had to be bad and hopped on the first plane home. I saw people I knew, asked them if they'd heard anything. Everyone was in the dark. It was frustrating.

The loss of eighty-four lives came as a real shock to the community, and a smack in the face to those of us who were young and new to the industry, a wake-up call to the dangers of offshore drilling. When the rig first came here, the perception was that it was big stuff. It was the largest semi-submersible in the world. Mobil Oil and ODECO could do no wrong. Those were the days of the Mobil and Gulf options, guys mortgaging their house so they could invest in the stock market. Back then you could fly out for the day, like it was a vacation or holiday. We were so naïve.

There was an organization here in town, the Oilfield Technical Society, which was mostly a social thing, a good way of mixing incoming mainlanders and foreigners with us locals. Mel Freid was one of the guys I knew working on the *Ranger*. He and I had been in a fraternity on the Memorial University campus, Delta, Beta, Sigma. That's going back a long time, forty years, maybe. We weren't close buddies— we happened to know one another from living here in St. John's, one of a few guys I'd gotten to know better through my involvement with OTS—and it would be doing him an injustice to say we were close. But I went to Mel's funeral as a friend and as executor of the organization. Media from all over the world were lined up along the snowbanks, shooting down as we left the service grieving. They stood up between the cars with their cameras stuck up in our faces. We felt like spitting on them.

The Newfoundland and Labrador Oil and Gas Industries Association really weren't representing the industry back then, OTS was. When the *Ocean Ranger* sank, the board decided we had to somehow recognize the magnitude of the tragedy and its impact on the community. A monument was chosen.

We'd all gone to the funerals and the service at the Basilica, but none of us had lost a brother, son or husband, and it was impossible for the committee to interpret what those people were going through. We knew it had to be done in conjunction with the *Ocean Ranger* Families Foundation. Lorraine Michael and Cle Newhook, God bless their souls, made sure what we were doing was done properly and that no one would be offended. Nothing was done without their consultation.

Choosing the proper location became a serious problem. Several of us thought Signal Hill would be appropriate because it overlooked the ocean and stood for security. Parks Canada wouldn't hear of it. We pulled as many strings as we could—I even went to Ottawa to plead our case—but they just wouldn't hear of it. I thought, *Jesus, fifty-six Newfoundlanders went down on that rig and we can't put something up there to honour them because Parks Canada, not Parks Newfoundland, says so?* Everyone was disgusted with the whole thing.

At the same time, the Provincial Government was talking about a monument park on the property across from Confederation Building, which would include an interpretation centre and garden. They'd even gone so far as to commission designs. While the concept was good, it never got off the ground. In hindsight, I'm glad things worked out the way they did because the importance of the *Ranger* memorial would've been lost amongst the dozen others.

I went to see Haig Young, a prominent cabinet minister from Harbour Grace. I explained our situation and a site was chosen almost immediately on what is now known as Confederation Hill.

We looked around for a landscape architect—a call went out in *The Evening Telegram*; everyone from ten-year-olds to victim's families responded with suggestions—and we finally decided on Fred Hand. Although it was his first commission, his ideas captured the essence of what we were trying to accomplish. For us, he could make it happen. He gave us the overall theme of two contrasting feelings—exposure to the elements, and comfort and solace—and created a comprehensive memorial site rather than a traditional monument. When it's blowing a gale up on that hill, it's really blowing a gale—you can almost feel what it was like that night on the Grand Banks—but as you walk in along the tree-lined and enclosed area towards the bronze plaque with the names of the eighty-four men placed against the cedar wall, the focal point, it gives you a sense of peace.

A sculptor from Ferryland, mentored by Gerry Squires, designed the monument, a massive abstract anchor. It dominates the view, and standing at the proper location you can see the Atlantic Ocean in the background.

In the fall of 1984, the final drawings were approved by the Families Foundation, and an agreement was signed with the Province to provide perpetual maintenance and assist in the construction.

The project wasn't going to come cheap: $172,000. We raised $12,000, which had accumulated some interest, but we were far short. The oil companies gave us as per their shares in Hibernia. Even ODECO donated $45,000. We tried to bum some money from ManuLife, the insurance company who held most of the policies for those working offshore, but the miserable bastards just gave us $3,000.

I'd known John Crosbie for a lot of years—he was a friend of the family and had attended my wedding in 1974. At the time, he was a federal cabinet minister. We had a casual meeting.

"John, we're trying to pull this off but we're really struggling. We need money."

"Leave it with me." That was all that he said.

This was 1985. It was three years after the *Ranger* sank—the Royal Commission was in full swing—and we wanted to give it some time.

Out of the blue, John called. "You got it."

"Got what?" I asked.

He laughed. "I got you your $25,000."

July 10, 1985, the memorial site was unveiled and blessed. It was a gorgeous summer day. I was the master of ceremonies and all spiffed off in a brand new light summer suit. Knowing most of the families would be there and that, for them, it would be a very sombre occasion and a lot of tears shed, I asked my wife "Is this suit too flashy or bright?" It's strange how you remember those silly little things from such important points in your life.

For many families, there was no body—there were just the twenty-two. Several people came up and thanked us, because now they finally had a place to go on a birthday or an anniversary. I thought, *At least they can now grieve in peace.*

I still walk up to Confederation Hill a few times a year, sometimes on the anniversary, sometimes just to snoop around and make sure the grounds are being maintained. When it's not February but the middle of August and I find a wreath or flowers or a picture, it's gratifying to know it's still an important place in people's lives. You do some things in your life, and you do other things. Regardless of how hard it came, in the end, putting together the monument gave the committee members a really good feeling inside.

Photo courtesy of Brian Bursey

ODECO electrician Paul Bursey. An album full of photos was never returned to his family by their American lawyer. This is one of the few which still exist.

WHY REMEMBERING IS STILL SO IMPORTANT
Brian, a brother

Paul and I were only a year apart, but as we began our professional lives he went one way and I went another. He became an electrician while I became a teacher. Once he received his apprenticeship, he decided to go out West. I got married in 1978 and settled down.

My mother was living alone—Dad had long since passed away—and because Paul was never in one place for too long and always coming and going, he continued living with her when he was home.

Whenever he was back in town we'd spend a lot of time together—it was a regular routine. We were at the point in our lives—I was twenty-nine and he was thirty—where family was beginning to have more of an importance. I like to think that he would've stayed home if he'd had the opportunity. It just didn't present itself at that particular time.

When he started working offshore in January 1980, he never planned on doing it for any great length of time, and still had his sights set out West. He wasn't intent on making a living out of it. The way he figured it, working on the Grand Banks was the type of experience that'd look good on a resume.

When he went out a week before the *Ranger* sank, that was supposed to be his last hitch. I can't remember exactly where he was headed, probably Alberta or northern British Columbia, but he already had his airline ticket purchased.

I've often thought about that night and how events unfolded: the smashed porthole, sea water washing over the ballast control panel, and the rig listing. As an electrician, I'm sure Paul was there with those other guys trying to fix things. It must've been pretty tough knowing they were losing her and that everything was slipping away from them. *What in the name of God do we do?* To me, it was a hard, hard death.

His body was never recovered. It was most difficult on my mother—there was no closure for her, or for any of us. We've all dealt with death; closure comes with a service and burial. We never got that and kept on wondering and wondering and thinking that one day he'd just walk in through the door.

What made it worse was that only a few weeks after the rig went down, my wife found out she was pregnant with our second child. My brother would now never share in that experience with us. Our son was born in October. We named him Paul. It was a fitting tribute, I guarantee, because he was the spit of him. Strangely, I sometimes think it was meant to be. Maybe I read too much into it, but when you see him, his actions and the way he does things, I see my brother. I can't help but feel that way. Even today, people say, "My God, he reminds me of Paul."

In that way, we have a living memory of him.

But we still never had a place where we could go, to mourn.

I used to say to my mother that we should have something to note his passing at the family plot in Mt. Carmel Cemetery. She couldn't because it meant she would have to finally admit that he was truly gone forever.

For years, I taught at Gonzaga. As a Catholic school, we often held general masses at St. Pius X for the entire student body, including a service dedicated to those of our greater family who'd lost their lives. For instance, if you were a student and your grandmother died and you wanted her remembered her name would be read aloud.

That was back before 1982.

When the rig sank, the five Gonzaga alumni who went down on her became the focal point of that mass.

Paul was one of those five.

As the years went by, more and more family members not necessarily related to those guys began turning up at the service and phoning the school asking whether or not it would be held. It soon got to the point where remembering the eighty-four seemed most appropriate, and we started making announcements in the local media and church bulletins.

With nothing marking the anniversary, no official day of mourning, it became the only tangible way of remembering, and it offered at least some solace to a lot of people. I know it helped my family.

It's even more important now when our history isn't being taught in schools like it once was. When I was teaching Newfoundland Culture, the *Ocean Ranger* disaster was something I made a point of introducing in my lectures, not because I had a personal interest, but because we had this massive Hibernia platform under construction at Bull Arm and we still didn't know a whole lot about the oil industry, something

I felt my students needed to be made keenly aware of. Part of that was a picture I had of the *Ranger* which at one time had hung in the foyer of the old Ports Canada Building. When the new building went up it was removed. Someone suggested they pass it along to us, and I asked for it to be put in my classroom. It was so massive that when I first got it I found myself staring at the men working on the deck—you could see the clothes they were wearing, almost make out a face. That's why most of the committee members said it would be too hard on a lot of the families if we were to include it in the service. I think they were right.

None of the current student body was alive in 1982, and the service gives them a chance to learn about a tragic part of our history. Years and years ago, we started a historical re-enactment to show how events unfolded through Sunday evening when the winds began to blow, Monday morning with the abandonment, the loss of radio contact, and then the nothingness, the emptiness. We did it in such a way that we were acutely aware of the families reliving it each and every day of their lives, every February. We didn't want to make it more difficult for them. We made it tactful, like a history lesson.

One of the most important parts of the service is the reflection from a student. The committee has always sought out someone to present their feelings on what the disaster means to them. Sometimes it's about the enormity of it, sometimes the impact on the community. Some talk about our tragic relationship with the sea, or how offshore oil development is our future, their future, with the hope that we have learned from past mistakes.

I still run into former students that went through with me—a scattered person might've had an uncle on board, one had a father, but most never had any connection—and it's something they always remember, something they hold special because they actively participated and learned through expression, instead of being made to just sit there and listen.

That's all so important if we're to keep the memory alive.

At the end of the service, an announcement is made for any family member who wants to come up and receive a candle lit in remembrance of their lost loved one. There's always a long line-up which still continues to grow. This past year over thirty people came up. A procession then makes its way to Confederation Hill, where a wreath and an attached note from the Gonzaga students and staff is laid at the memorial site. In the past twenty-seven years, I can't remember many days where we've had fine weather—it's always been cold and windy, like it always is in mid-February, like it was back then.

I've done a lot of interviews, especially in the early years, but not so much anymore. I was glad to see interest pick up again on the twenty-fifth anniversary. For us, the families, that was the big one—the milestone. The memorial service committee talked about doing something special, bringing in someone from the oil industry or maybe government. But where were they all these years? Nowhere, that's where. In the end, we decided not to change a thing. I think that's what people like about it most, its simplicity.

Even though I'm retired, the school still calls me to help organize the event. This past February, a few of them asked, now that twenty-five years have passed, if it's time for Gonzaga to bow out. *Is there really anything else we can do?* We talked about it amongst the leading members of staff and the school administration, and everyone felt that the need was certainly still there. There's no formal group any longer, the *Ocean Ranger* Families Foundation is long gone—the one real connection we had to one another—and as we move to the point at which the public begins to forget, a whole new generation of students is coming along who need to know.

The core group of teachers who were members of the original committee have retired and moved on and have been replaced. It makes me wonder if the new staff will have the same interest, take on and form an opinion, and make it a point to have the service for the families, to offer them a place to come together and continue to heal. That's why it's still so important, to remember the eighty-four, men like my brother, Paul.

To remember what we have lost.

EPILOGUE, OR ABOUT FINDING COURAGE

One of my earliest memories is of the house being quiet and still. The phone rang and my mother rushed upstairs to answer it. I mentioned this to her years later and she recalled it vividly. It was February 15, 1982. Calling was my grandmother to talk about what everyone was talking about that Monday, the *Ocean Ranger*. "At bus stops on the steep, snowbanked streets leading down to the harbour, on the job, in classrooms, shopping centres and bars," Wednesday's edition of *The Daily News* read, "people spoke of how the sea had once more claimed its toll."

In the morning, and even as the day wore on, there was a lot of hope for survivors. But as the awful images of the capsized lifeboat splashed across the evening news, the harbinger of ultimate doom, that hope turned to resignation and defeat. My father's cousin, Ron, was out there then. His family was one of the lucky few, if I could use such an adjective to describe what was, for them, the most devastating of tragedies, in that his body was one of the twenty-two recovered.

It's because of his story that I wrote this book and spent the better part of two years researching and compiling stories.

The first interviewee I contacted was a former Universal Helicopter pilot, the company contracted to shuttle men to and from the rig. In my mind, there were images of the chopper getting blown across the tarmac, and then flying out through gale-force winds only to find nothingness at the drill site. The prospect of writing about that was exciting. But when I went to his house and rang the doorbell, no one answered. That night, I left a message on his voice mail and another the following week. I never heard from him again.

With such a daunting task ahead of me, it was a disconcerting experience.

I wondered whether or not enough time had passed. The twenty-fifth anniversary resurrected a lot of painful memories. The iconic images of the *Hudson* unloading its dreadful cargo at Pier 17, and the raised rig's massive submarine-like pontoons breaking the ocean's surface about to be scuttled, were once again on the front pages of the papers. Played and replayed on radio and television was Rick Flynn's hollow voice calling to the rig that final time: "*Ocean Ranger...* Jack, are you there?" For many, it was like 1982 all over again.

If I was looking for an answer, I found it at the Holy Sepulchre Cemetery on Topsail Road. Most of the Heffernans are buried there, including Ron. Growing up, I'd always thought of him as nineteen or twenty when he died. I'm not sure why, other than my mother said he had been young. That's why I was so surprised to learn he'd gone out to Edmonton with his brother, Ray, and was in the process of a divorce, a lot for such a young life. I wasn't prepared for what I saw. He'd been twenty-eight—my age then.

There were two other graves a stone's throw from his, both *Ocean Ranger* victims.

Is this the oil boom? I asked myself.

Certainly not a lot had changed since the *Ranger* sank. Guys like me, like Ron, were still leaving in droves to head out West to the Promised Land, to Alberta, in the hopes of making a life for themselves, while the government puffed its proverbial chest about how oil, about how Hibernia, Hebron and White Rose, was our economic salvation. The old political rhetoric of "have not will be no more" was chic yet again.

I thought I understood what the cost of prosperity meant. I'd read the Royal Commission's findings, local newspapers, watched the CBC reports, I'd done all those things my university professors had taught me historians do. I thought I understood.

"As soon as the snow starts falling, I think of him," Elaine, Ron's sister, said, tears streaming down her grief-stricken face. I hadn't seen anything like that until then.

I realized there was no way I could express her feelings with my own words, or what it was like to get off the chopper on Thursday and on Monday find out that all of your friends were dead, to face the stark reality of raising your unborn child alone, to have to pack up and put away your son's clothes because he wasn't coming home anymore, to never get the chance to say goodbye. Only their voices and their memories could do that.

Along the way, there were a lot of kind faces and open doors. People wanted to tell their story, one that has been with us for as long as we have cast our nets from this rock: tragedy at sea. Part of my job was to inform a whole new generation who knew nothing of the indelible mark the disaster has left on our collective psyche. But for those directly impacted, facts were unimportant, facts were not personal truth. What I really wanted to share were their experiences and precious feelings. This is a book about memory and emotion, not history. I've sat in dozens of living rooms, at kitchen tables and in coffee shops, offices and boardrooms. I stood where John O'Brien stood outside the CBC entrance with his head held low; I sat in an office high above Water Street overlooking the harbour, wind and rain slashing at the windows, while I was told about the depths of the rig. I've seen photo albums full of young men who never came home, read letters they wrote their wives from the rig, seen the check marks on the crew manifest beside the names of those who'd been found and identified.

I guess you could say I've travelled among other people's pain: rig workers, victims' families, emergency responders, priests, government officials and reporters. They are all ordinary people, many of them from very different backgrounds but connected by the scar left from the longest week of their lives, talking about something so traumatic that it often defies words.

But rather than sadness and defeat, I found in them courage, the need to overcome and find meaning in tragedy, that ineffable thing that makes us the unique people that we are, Newfoundlanders.

ACKNOWLEDGEMENTS

The source material for this book was almost fifty interviews. I'm indebted to those who kindly agreed to them, especially to those whose stories were not included but which helped me to understand.

Many people offered invaluable assistance, but one deserves special thanks. A sounding board throughout the entire process, Gerard Collins was constantly there with input and kind words of reassurance.

I'm lucky to have some very special people in my life, too: Lesley, for loving me; Darren, for being more than a friend; Anja, my daughter, for teaching me about life.

For trusting my vision: Donna Francis and Creative Book Publishing.

A lot of people were more than helpful: Marie Wadden, Ed Kavanagh, Lisa Moore, Michelle Butler Hallett, Ramona Dearing, Jacob Fergus, Geoff Meeker, Frank Kennedy, Dick Green, Burton Janes, Brenda Green, Wilson Russell, Ted Blades, Heather Elliot, Nellie Strowbridge, Sturla Gunnarsson, Valerie Kent, Bruce Dyke, Karla Hayward, Danette Dooley, Steve Porter, David Whelan, Don Sedgwick, Joan Sullivan, Mark Callanan, David Benson and RN Wagner.

Several organizations were also supportive: Writer's Alliance of Newfoundland and Labrador, St. John's Arts Grants Council, CBC, Centre for Newfoundland Studies, *NL Quarterly* and *Riddle Fence*.

All material is based on interviews conducted by the author, excluding:

"The Darkness of a Little House" by Cris Sonntag and Mike Heffernan

"Two Monologues About Being Young: Part 1" by Barbara Yaffee and Mike Heffernan

Acknowledgements:

"A Unique Bond" first appeared as "The Longest Week" in *Riddle Fence*. No. 2. September, 2008.

"The Most Dangerous Part of the Rig" first appeared as "Madhouse" in *The Newfoundland Quarterly*. Vol. 100, No. 3. July, 2008.